COUSCOUS RECIPES BOOK

The Best-ever of Couscous Cookbook

(A Yummy Couscous Cookbook You Will Need)

Terri Agostini

Published by Alex Howard

© **Terri Agostini**

All Rights Reserved

Couscous Recipes Book: The Best-ever of Couscous Cookbook (A Yummy Couscous Cookbook You Will Need)

ISBN 978-1-990169-90-8

All rights reserved. No part of this guide may be reproduced in any form without permission in writing from the publisher except in the case of brief quotations embodied in critical articles or reviews.

Legal & Disclaimer

The information contained in this book is not designed to replace or take the place of any form of medicine or professional medical advice. The information in this book has been provided for educational and entertainment purposes only.

The information contained in this book has been compiled from sources deemed reliable, and it is accurate to the best of the Author's knowledge; however, the Author cannot guarantee its accuracy and validity and cannot be held liable for any errors or omissions. Changes are periodically made to this book. You must consult your doctor or get professional medical advice before using any of the suggested remedies, techniques, or information in this book.

Table of contents

Part 1 1
Introduction 2
Moroccan Couscous With Seven Vegetables 4
Saffa Medfouna Recipe 6
Couscous With Beef And Vegetables – Authentic Moroccan Delicacy 8
Vegetarian Moroccan Couscous Recipe 10
Couscous With Lamb & Vegetables 12
Couscous With Harvest Vegetables 14
Harissa Couscous Salad With A Twist Of Roasted Tomatoes 16
Minted Harissa Couscous With Shrimps 18
Moroccan Salad, Couscous, And Raisins 20
A Moroccan Delicacy - Chicken Harissa Soup With Couscous 22
Moroccan-Style Vegetable Couscous 24
Couscous With Quick Preserved Lemon 26
Moroccan Tofu With Couscous 28
Apricots And Pistachio With Grilled Chicken Couscous 30
Moroccan Seafood Stew With Couscous 32
Moroccan Chicken Couscous 34
Moroccan Tilapia With Couscous 36

Moroccan Peanut Couscous With Peas 38

Moroccan Chicken, Apricot And Almond Tagine (With Couscous) 40

Quick Moroccan Couscous 42

Moroccan Spiced Vegetable Couscous 44

Moroccan Chicken With Buttered Couscous 46

Spiced Lamb Chops With Couscous 48

Moroccan-Style Chickpea Stew 50

Aromatic Moroccan Couscous Recipe 52

Breakfast 54

Honeyed Couscous Pudding 55

Breakfast Couscous With Dried Fruit Compote 57

Couscous Muffins Recipe 59

Couscous Fritters With Feta 62

Main Course 64

Moroccan Couscous With Seven Vegetables 65

Chorizo Beef And Couscous Stuffed Peppers 70

Couscous Flat Breads 73

Ginger Soy Israeli Couscous With Baby Bok Choy 75

Salad 77

Mediterranean Couscous Salad 78

Couscous Salad 80

Part 2 82

- Introduction 83
- Meat And Seven Vegetable Couscous 85
- Chicken Couscous, Chickpeas And Raisins 88
- Couscous Of Flap With Tfaya Conger 90
- Lamb Couscous With Cardoons 93
- Couscous With Onions, Tomatoes And Broad Beans 95
- Mushroom Couscous 98
- Seafood Couscous 101
- Couscous With Prunes And Lamb 104
- Chicken Couscous With Apples 106
- Three Meat Royal Couscous 109
- Lentil Couscous With Vegetables 112
- Cinnamon Sweet Couscous 114
- Beef And Vegetable Couscous 116
- Chicken Peas And Pumpkin Couscous 119
- Tfaya Couscous With Chicken And Caramelized Onions ... 122
- Moroccan Couscous With Nuts 125
- Dried Fruit Couscous 127
- Roasted Lamb Couscous 130
- Delicious Couscous Recipes 133
- Recipe 1: Garlic Shrimp And Couscous 133
- Recipe 2: Roasted Pumpkin Couscous Dish 136
- Recipe 3: Couscous Cakes For Everyone 138

Recipe 4: Fried Couscous Nuggets 141

Recipe 5: Tangy And Sweet Couscous With White Fish 143

Recipe 6: Baked Stuffed Peppers With Couscous 146

Recipe 7: Fried Couscous With Green Veggies 148

Recipe 8: Chicken Couscous Entree 150

Recipe 9: Stuffed Chicken With Couscous And Sundried Tomatoes 152

Recipe 10: Spicy Couscous Soup 154

Recipe 11: Sweet Potatoes With Awesome Couscous Inside 157

Recipe 12: Tomato-Based Couscous Awesome Dish 159

Recipe 13: Artichoke And Lemon Yummy Couscous Dish ... 161

Recipe 14: Cheese, Peas And Couscous 164

Recipe 15: Gratin Couscous 167

Recipe 16: Healthy Couscous And Chickpea Casserole 170

Recipe 17: Very Simple Couscous Recipe 172

Recipe 18: Chinese Fried Couscous 174

Recipe 19: Mushrooms And Broccoli Couscous Side Dish ... 176

Recipe 20: Scallops And Couscous Perfect Dish 178

Recipe 21: Quiche-Like Couscous Recipe 180

Recipe 22: Butternut Squash And Couscous Together 182

Recipe 23: Awesome Couscous And Orange Cake 184

Recipe 24: Cold Couscous Greek Salad 186

Recipe 25: Simply Delicious Moroccan Couscous Dish.......... 188

Part 1

Introduction

Moroccan food is loved by a diversity of people around the Globe, and due to their increasing demand, the trend of Moroccan restaurants and dishes is growing as well. Let it be Thanksgiving or any ordinary meal, Moroccan cuisine, especially couscous, is always on the table.

This book presents 25 popular Moroccan couscous recipes which are delicious, as well as nutritious. Please note that the ingredients and directions mentioned are standardized for the number of people mentioned in each recipe. If you have a variable craving for any particular ingredient, or you need to serve in different quantities, you can alter the recipe accordingly.

These recipes contain an array of ingredients, and you have to ensure that you have all of them available before starting to make any dish. A lot of people compromise on one or two ingredients, and that is where they lose the authentic taste of Moroccan couscous. It is all about flavors and richness that you ought to experience in every chunk.

It does not matter whether you are a vegetarian or not. This Book caters to the requirements and choices of each individual to an equal extent. You will find recipes that are best for meat lovers and a couple of recipes that are best for veggie-lovers.

If you happen to be a meat-lover, you could add a lot of variations to the recipes mentioned below by using different kinds of meat. For instance, roast and grilled chicken lovers can always add the form of chicken they prefer, instead of using boiled meat. Even though the quantity of ingredients required for couscous is quite a lot, it is not difficult to prepare any of the dishes mentioned in this Book.

Moroccan Couscous With Seven Vegetables

In Morocco, couscous happens to be a proper name for a time-honored stew which is laced with veggies, flavors, and ground spices of North Africa. This is a delicious party dish which is easy to make.

Servings: **6**

Ingredients
- A large onion
- Beef or lamb (600g)
- Olive oil (2 tablespoons)
- 300 g of turnip
- Couscous (4 cups, dried)
- Chickpeas (250g)
- A teaspoon of turmeric
- A tablespoon of salt
- ½ teaspoon black pepper
- Coriander bouquet (1)
- Pinch of saffron
- Tomatoes (2)
- Small cabbage

- A teaspoon of ginger
- A large sweet potato
- 300g butternut
- 3 carrots
- Courgettes (200g)

Directions

- Take a large casserole to heat olive oil
- Add spices, salt, meat, pepper and tomatoes and heat further for about 10 minutes
- Add chickpeas and 1.5 liters of water
- Let it boil and simmer for about 50 minutes
- Prepare the veggies and keep them aside
- Add turnip, coriander, and cabbage in the broth and let it bubble for about 35 minutes
- Place the lid for another 20 minutes after adding potatoes
- Flip in the butternut and courgettes
- Use tongs to remove meat from casserole and cut into pieces before serving

Saffa Medfouna Recipe

This is yet another famous Moroccan dish that caters to the taste buds of beef, lamb or chicken lovers. The meat is hidden under the dome of steamed couscous which enhances the taste as well.

Serves: 6 people

Ingredients

(For seffa)

- A cup of powdered sugar
- Vegetable oil (3 tablespoons)
- Salt (2 tsp.)
- 4 tbsp. butter
- 2 pounds couscous
- A cup of golden raisins
- Butter (4 tbsp.)
- A cup of powdered sugar

(For meat)

- A whole chicken
- Sweet onions (2)
- A tablespoon of ginger
- Half a teaspoon of black pepper
- A teaspoon of white pepper
- $1/4^{th}$ of a cup olive oil
- Butter (4 tbsp.)
- Cinnamon sticks (2 pieces, small)
- A teaspoon of turmeric

- A teaspoon of saffron
- Salt (1 tsp.)
- Cilantro (1/4 cup)

(For seffa)

- Cinnamon (2 tbsp.)
- Almonds (half a cup)
- Powdered sugar (a cup)

Directions

- Add salt water in a couscoussier
- Let it boil and simmer
- Steam the couscous thrice
- Add raisins in 3rd steaming
- Mix oil, onions, meat, cilantro, butter and spices in a pot. Brown the meat for about 10 minutes. Cover your pot and cook until the chicken is tender. When cooked, reduce the liquids until a thick sauce is formed.
- Toss the couscous with butter and sugar
- Place one-third of the mixture on serving dish
- Arrange chicken in center and cover with sauce, together with couscous on top of chicken

Couscous With Beef And Vegetables – Authentic Moroccan Delicacy

The perfect stew made up of beef and veggies offers a bud-recharging combination for foodies. The slow process of making this dish ensures that the couscous is well prepared and filled with the smell of meat.

Serves: 6

Ingredients

Spices

- 2 teaspoons of salt
- A teaspoon of coriander
- A teaspoon of turmeric
- A pinch of saffron
- A teaspoon of cumin
- 2 teaspoons of ginger
- Pepper (1 teaspoon)
- A teaspoon of cumin
- A teaspoon of paprika

Stew

- 2 pounds of chicken or lamb

- 4 cups of water
- 2 tablespoons of olive oil
- Garlic (a teaspoon, mined)
- A chopped onion
- Tomato sauce (a cup)
- Bell pepper (1/2)
- A zucchini
- A cup of tomato sauce
- 2 carrots
- A can of chickpeas
- A medium potato and one yellow squash

Couscous

- Water (3 cups)
- $1/4^{th}$ of a cup butter
- 2 cups of couscous
- Chicken base (4 teaspoons)

Directions

- Add spices to a dish and leave it for a while
- Chop meat and brown it for 5 minutes in oil
- Add garlic and onion. Cook for 5 minutes
- Add tomato sauce, water, and spices. Cook for about 10 minutes
- Add potato and carrots to cook for 10 more minutes
- Toss in zucchini, chickpeas and bell pepper to cook for about 30 minutes.
- Add couscous to boiling water and leave for 5 minutes

Vegetarian Moroccan Couscous Recipe

This is a super easy, delicious and nutritious dish that is easy to make. Moreover, it caters to the cravings of vegetarians. Plus, this dish nests flavors from all across North Africa. So brace yourself!

Serves: 6

Ingredients

- Garlic (2 teaspoons, chopped)
- Tomato paste (2 tbsp.)
- A medium sweet onion
- ½ teaspoon cinnamon
- Olive oil (1.5 tbsp.)
- Ginger (1/4th of a teaspoon)
- A tablespoon of harissa
- ¼ cup of cilantro
- 2.5 cups of vegetable broth
- A pound of zucchini
- 2 pounds of sweet potatoes
- 4 medium carrots
- Apricots (dried, 1/3rd of a cup)
- Cabbage (shredded, 3 cups)
- Salt and pepper as required
- 10 ounces of couscous
- ¼ cup of golden raisins
- Chickpeas (between 1.5 and 2 cups)

Directions

- Take a large pot to heat the oil
- Toss in onion and garlic and heat until softened
- Add ginger, harissa, tomato paste, cinnamon and half a cup of broth before boiling
- Toss in carrots, apricots, cilantro, raisins, cabbage, zucchini and potatoes to stir and combine
- Add remaining broth and boil
- Season with pepper and salt
- Cover the pot
- Allow it to simmer for another hour
- Add chickpeas and simmer for 10 more minutes
- Pour in the couscous you have prepared meanwhile

Couscous With Lamb & Vegetables

This recipe yields plumper and fluffy couscous due to prolonged time and typical method of steaming. The grains are also tender which proves that the extra effort is worth it.

Serves: 5-6

Ingredients

- A can of chickpeas
- 1 zucchini
- A tomato
- A teaspoon of salt
- One and a half teaspoons of garlic
- Saltwater
- A pound of lamb meat
- 2 carrots and parsnips, each
- A teaspoon of ginger
- A potato and a can of chickpeas
- Serano pepper (1)
- Half a squash
- 2 teaspoons of cumin

- An onion (medium)
- Vegetable broth or water
- A bunch of parsley
- A teaspoon of pepper

Directions

- Peel and cut all veggies
- Take a couscousierre to add parsnips, potato, sweet potato, lamb, tomato, pepper, onion, carrots, and squash
- Pour in the broth
- Mix the ingredients and toss in the parsley bouquet
- Let it boil
- Spread the grains in a bowl and half a cup salt water to separate them before steaming the couscous
- Add the couscous to the top of couscousiere
- Turn on the stove
- Cover the pot and heat for about 20 minutes
- If the grains feel dry, transfer into the bowl
- Steam and wet the grains for 3 times
- Add zucchini and chickpeas in 3rd steaming
- Dump the grains on a serving plate
- Pour the remaining liquid into the dish and serve after arranging

Couscous With Harvest Vegetables

This fantastic dish takes about 40 minutes to prepare and please note that you could even use a homemade Harissa paste as a sideline. The fragrance of harvest veggies sparks up a strong craving.

Serves: 4 to 6

Ingredients

- 4 links to lamb sausage
- Olive oil (approx.. 2 tablespoons)
- 5 cups lamb broth
- Fresh mint leaves/cilantro
- A teaspoon of smoked paprika and cinnamon, each
- 10 ounces of couscous
- A teaspoon of salt
- A red onion
- Garlic cloves (4)
- Ginger root (a tablespoon, grated)
- 4 Summer squash and carrots, each
- A cup of golden raisins
- A young zucchini
- 2 turnips
- A can of chickpeas

Directions

- Heat oil in a large skillet
- Toss in sausage and sauté for 5 minutes

- Add onion and garlic before sautéing for another 5 minutes
- Add turnips, ¾ teaspoon of salt and carrots to stir and blend
- Add cinnamon, smoked paprika and ginger into the mixture and stir thoroughly
- Add lamb broth and let it boil
- Lower the heat of your stove
- Allow it to simmer for 20 minutes
- Add zucchini and chickpeas while stirring with other ingredients.
- It should simmer for another 10 minutes
- Toss in the raisins and heat to a mild simmer while you prepare the couscous as per instructions on your respective packaging
- Fluff it with fork
- Add couscous, vegetables, and sausage in a bowl to serve

Harissa Couscous Salad With A Twist Of Roasted Tomatoes

It is a very flavorsome recipe that is quite well-known for its versatility. The fragrance and chunks of almonds, roasted tomatoes, parsley, mint and garlic yogurt sauce are something that no one can forget after eating.

Serves: 4

Ingredients

- A tablespoon of harissa
- 3 tablespoons of olive oil
- Flaked almond (toasted, 50g)
- A can of chickpeas
- 12 tomatoes
- 3 onions
- A garlic clove
- A tablespoon of tahini paste
- 200 grams of couscous
- Parsley (half a small pack)

- Greek-style yogurt (4 tablespoons)
- Mint (half a pack)

Directions

- Heat the oven to 200 degrees Celsius
- Add 2 tablespoons of oil, tomatoes, and harissa
- Season in a roasting tin
- Bake for 45 minutes
- Take a large frying pan to heat the remaining oil
- Toss onions and sizzle for a couple of minutes
- Cook for 15 minutes
- Take a bowl to mix tahini paste, garlic, seasoning, and yogurt
- Add couscous to a large bowl
- Add 400ml of boiling water
- Let it absorb water
- Fork the chickpeas, herbs, onions and almonds
- Add tomatoes and onions at the top

Minted Harissa Couscous With Shrimps

If you like, you can even broil the shrimps or grill them. It is entirely up to you. Shrimps are also used as appetizers. You could thread them on individual skewers as well and lose the couscous.

Serves: 4

Ingredients

- A cup of couscous
- A pound of shrimp
- Mint leaves
- 4 tomatoes
- 2 tablespoons of harissa
- A tablespoon of lemon zest
- A teaspoon of ground cumin
- Olive oil (1/4th of a cup)
- A teaspoon of kosher salt

Directions

- Turn on the stove and let the grill to about 450 degrees
- Combine harissa, zest, cumin, oil, salt and lemon juice in a bowl
- Add shrimp in a bowl
- Toss with sauce and leave for 20 minutes
- Thread shrimp on skewers
- Prepare couscous as mentioned
- Add remaining zest in the couscous

- Fluff with fork
- Stir in a tablespoon of lemon juice and oil with half a teaspoon salt
- Brush tomatoes with oil
- Grill tomatoes and shrimp for 4 minutes
- Serve couscous with a sprinkle of mint, sauce, and salt

Moroccan Salad, Couscous, And Raisins

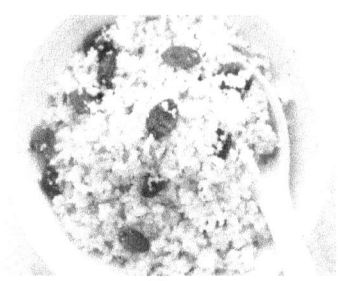

This dish is not only delicious, but it cooks very quickly if compared with other recipes. If preferred, you could add more raisins. Since this recipe does not feature meat by default, you could chicken as well if you like. It all depends on your preference.

Serves: 4

Ingredients

- ¼ teaspoon ground cinnamon
- A cup of couscous
- ¼ cup pine nuts (roasted)
- Half a teaspoon turmeric
- A teaspoon of salt
- A tablespoon of butter (unsalted)
- $1/4^{th}$ teaspoon ground cumin
- One-fourth cup seedless raisins (dark)

Directions

- Take a three quarter saucepan

- Toss in salt, cinnamon, raisins, butter cumin and turmeric in 1 ¼ cups of water
- Let it boil
- Stir in couscous
- Take it off the stove
- Toss in pine nuts and cover
- Leave it for about 5 minutes
- Use a fork to fluff the couscous
- Place in a serving bowl

A Moroccan Delicacy - Chicken Harissa Soup With Couscous

It can also be used for watery soups and for filling soups as well. When you cook it in soup, it has the tendency to absorb the aromatic richness.

Serves: 4

Ingredients

- 2 onions
- A teaspoon of harissa
- A tablespoon of tomato paste
- 2.62 pounds of chicken
- A carrot
- 6 cups of water
- Half a teaspoon ground cumin
- Half celeriac
- Half a cup couscous
- 2 cups of tinned tomatoes
- A teaspoon of sugar and paprika, each
- A cinnamon stick
- 2 tablespoons of parsley
- Salt
- 2 tablespoons of cilantro
- Lemon juice
- 2 tablespoons of mint
- Black pepper
- 2 tablespoons of olive oil

Directions

- Take off the skin from chicken
- Make pieces and discard skin
- Pour olive oil into a pan and fry chicken pieces
- Take out chicken pieces; keep aside
- Toss in onions, carrot, and celeriac and cook for about 7 minutes; stir occasionally
- Sprinkle paprika, harissa, and veggies in the pan and mix with the vegetable mixture
- Place chicken pieces back into the pan
- Boil 4 cups of water
- Toss in cinnamon stick, tomatoes, sugar, and tomato paste
- Add pepper and salt before decreasing heat; let it bubble with closed lid for an hour
- Take the chicken pieces out of soup and shred
- Pour 2 cups of water in the pan
- Let it boil, then add couscous and stir
- Lower the temperature and throw in chopped herbs
- Let it cook for about 10 minutes
- Place chicken pieces back into the pan
- Drizzle lemon juice, salt, and pepper

Moroccan-Style Vegetable Couscous

This vegetarian recipe is for Moroccan Vegetable Couscous and is delicious, no doubt. But it can also be used as an accompaniment to any other Moroccan style dish. So grab your forks!

Serves: 6

Ingredients

- 2 teaspoons of garlic and tomato paste, each
- A medium sweet onion
- A tablespoon of harissa
- Extra virgin olive oil (1.5 tablespoons)
- Half a teaspoon cinnamon
- One-fourth of a teaspoon ginger
- 3 cups of cabbage
- 10 ounces of couscous
- Salt and black pepper
- ¼ cup golden raisins
- 2.5 cups vegetable broth
- 2 pounds sweet potatoes

- A pound of zucchini
- Cooked chickpeas (1 ¾ cups)
- ¼ cup cilantro
- 12 ounces carrots
- One-third of a cup dried apricots

Directions

- Take a large pot of heat olive oil
- Toss in onions and garlic and cook until softened
- Add cinnamon, tomato paste, harissa, vegetable broth, ginger, and let it boil
- Add cabbage, raisins, apricots, zucchini, potatoes, cabbage and cilantro to stir and mix
- Add remaining vegetable broth, salt, and pepper to boil more
- Simmer for an hour
- Toss in chickpeas and simmer for another 5 minutes
- Prepare couscous
- Toss couscous on a large platter and top with vegetable stew

Couscous With Quick Preserved Lemon

Here is yet another tasty recipe that recharges your taste buds due to the drizzling of preserved lemon! Isn't that amazing? Another great perk is that you could prepare this dish within half an hour and it serves about 6 people.

Serves: 6

Ingredients

- 4 lemons
- Pearl couscous (6 cups)
- Salt and pepper
- Cilantro leaves (2 cups)
- Water

Directions

- Prepare couscous (if it is instant, instructions are in the packet)
- For non-instant couscous, add it to a large bowl
- Fill 3/4th of the pot with water
- Boil
- Pour couscous in boiling water
- Cook for 8 minutes
- Drain the couscous and add cilantro and lemon
- Toss the pepper
- Sprinkle some salt
- Slice 2 lemons
- Put them on a plate

- Toss one and salt the other
- Stack on each other
- Leave in a baking dish for 20 minutes
- Rinse with cold water

Moroccan Tofu With Couscous

The seasoning of kosher salt together with Moroccan seasoning kicks in the mouth and revitalizes the taste buds every time you eat it. Eat it once, and you will develop a craving in no time.

Serves: 4

Ingredients

- A pound of package greens
- A cup of couscous
- Ground pepper
- Kosher salt
- 2 tablespoons of olive oil
- 1.5 teaspoons cumin
- 1/3 cup of apricots
- 12 to 14 ounces of a tofu package
- 15 ounces of cherry tomatoes
- A teaspoon of Moroccan seasoning
- A tablespoon of harissa
- 1/3 cup of green olives
- 2 tablespoons of fresh cilantro

Directions

- Peel the veggies and chop
- Take a pot of heat oil and toss in the vegetables to stir and cook for 5 minutes
- Add half a teaspoon cumin, pepper, Moroccan seasoning, tomato juice and salt and cook until thickened
- Add two cups of water
- Toss in tomatoes
- Simmer for 10 minutes
- Prepare couscous meanwhile as directed on packaging
- Add harissa, a teaspoon of cumin, half a teaspoon Moroccan seasoning and half a cup water. Now toss in tofu and apricots to warm for 5 minutes
- Chop the soup herbs
- Add in the pot with cilantro
- Sprinkle harissa and salt
- Present with couscous and remaining cilantro

Apricots And Pistachio With Grilled Chicken Couscous

The combination of pistachios and apricots and that too with a chicken couscous is truly amazing even if you are not a food lover. The kicking of salty and sweet flavors in your mouth together with Moroccan spices is indeed an experience to be remembered.

Serves: 4-6

Ingredients

- A teaspoon of kosher salt
- 2 cups balsamic vinegar
- Canola oil
- Lime zest
- 1/4 teaspoons of black pepper and cumin, each
- 1.5 cups of instant couscous
- ¼ cups of flat leaf parsley and fresh mint
- Half a cup pistachios
- 2 tablespoons of apricot jam
- 4 boneless chicken breasts
- Kosher salt
- Black pepper
- 6 apricots

Directions

- To prepare couscous, add 1.5 cups of water to boil
- Toss in salt, pepper, and cumin
- Let it absorb water for 5 minutes

- Transfer to a bowl
- Make it fluffy with fork
- Toss in lime zest and pistachios
- Add some parsley and mint
- To prepare apricot balsamic glaze, add vinegar in saucepan
- Cook until it is reduced to half a cup
- Whisk the jam and allow it to cool
- For apricot as well as chicken, heat charcoal for grilling
- Brush these two with oil and season with pepper and salt
- Grill the chicken for 9 minutes
- Leave for 5 minutes before slicing
- Grill the apricots and slice into wedges
- Transfer couscous to serving plate and arrange apricots, chicken while sprinkling the glaze

Moroccan Seafood Stew With Couscous

This dish is perfect to enjoy a relaxed dinner with friends, along with the beach or even in your dining room. It is fantastically easy to prepare even for the first-timers.

Serves: 4

Ingredients

- A cup of couscous
- 12 ounces of shrimp
- Ground pepper
- Kosher salt
- A tablespoon of paprika
- 26 ounces box of tomatoes (chopped)
- Half a cup olives (pitted)
- 2 tablespoon of olive oil
- An onion
- A tablespoon of ground cumin
- 8 ounces of green beans
- 2 pounds of mussels
- Half a cup cilantro

Directions

- Take a heatproof bowl to prepare couscous by following the instructions on your packaging
- Use a large pot to heat olive oil
- Toss in onion, a teaspoon of salt, paprika, and pepper to stir and cook for about 5-7 minutes
- Pour in half a cup water with tomatoes, cilantro, beans, brine, and olives
- Allow it to simmer
- Stir in mussels
- Cook for 5 minutes
- Add the shrimp
- Cook for another 5 minutes until the shrimp is opaque
- Fluff the couscous and divide

Moroccan Chicken Couscous

If you want to experience the richness of Moroccan spices while taking care of all the health aspects, this is the perfect dish for you. Since it does not even require much of ingredients, you could make it any night.

Serves: 4

Ingredients

- Half a cup fresh cilantro
- A cup of couscous
- Half a teaspoon cumin and cinnamon, each
- 2 carrots
- A large onion
- 2 tablespoons of olive oil
- Kosher salt
- Ground pepper
- A chicken breast (1/4 of a pound)
- Lemon zest (half a lemon)
- Juice of one lemon
- 15 ounces of canned chickpeas (no-salt)
- Apricots and prunes (1/4 cup)

Directions

- Take a saucepan to combine carrots and a cup of water
- Heat for 7 minutes
- Take a large skillet and heat

- Pour in olive oil and chicken after seasoning with pepper and salt
- Turn occasionally and cook for 4 minutes
- Transfer to a plate
- Toss in ¼ teaspoon salt and onion to the skillet
- Cover and cook for about 6 minutes
- Stir in cinnamon and cumin and remove from heat
- Add couscous, lemon zest, apricots and chickpeas to the skillet
- Now add carrots and cooking water
- Stir to combine and simmer
- Toss in chicken
- Cover and leave until the couscous is tender in about 5 minutes and the liquid is absorbed
- Fluff with a fork
- Drizzle lemon juice
- Sprinkle cilantro and salt

Moroccan Tilapia With Couscous

Tilapia fillets with a spicy sauce topping and a tender couscous. What else could be better than this flavorsome combination? This is particularly a good recipe if you are looking for something different as this recipe includes mint flavors together sourness of lemon and yogurt.

Serves: 4

Ingredients

- 1.5 cups of couscous (uncooked)
- A garlic clove
- A tablespoon of olive oil
- 4 tilapia fillets
- Half a teaspoon ground cumin and Hungarian paprika, each
- 2 tablespoons Greek yogurt
- 2 teaspoons of lemon juice
- Half a cup golden raisins
- ¼ cups of mint leaves

Directions

- To prepare sauce, take a small bowl and add two tablespoons of mint, garlic, paprika, lemon juice, yogurt, olive oil and cumin; mix thoroughly
- Take a large skillet and heat the remaining oil
- Apply pepper on fillets
- Place fillets in the skillet
- Apply heat 4 minutes on each side
- Use a saucepan to boil 2 2/3 cups of water
- Add couscous and raisins to it
- Stir gently
- Get it off the stove and leave for about 5 minutes
- Use a fork to fluff
- Toss in the remaining mint
- Transfer each fillet in serving plates
- Drizzle sauce on each fillet and serve with couscous

Moroccan Peanut Couscous With Peas

Here comes yet another super easy and delicious recipe with an incredibly low cooking time. Moreover, the combination of peanut couscous with peas is relatively newer for a lot of people, and you are going to love it.

Serves: 6

Ingredients

- 2 tablespoons of canola oil
- Salt
- Pepper
- Half a cup peanut butter
- Half a cup chopped onions
- 3 garlic cloves
- Half a teaspoon cumin
- Half a cup green or red bell pepper
- 1.5 cups chicken
- A cup of couscous
- 10 ounces of frozen peas

Directions

- Take a three-quarter saucepan to heat oil
- Toss in onion, garlic and bell pepper and cook until translucent
- Add broth and let it boil
- Toss in cumin and peanut butter and blend
- Add pepper and salt

- Now add peas and let it boil
- Stir the couscous and allow it to boil again while stirring
- Take it off the stove and leave for 5 minutes
- Fluff with a fork

Moroccan Chicken, Apricot And Almond Tagine (With Couscous)

This dish has a lot of going on! Just talk about tagine for a while, and it is crazy good! The sauces are quite heavily spiced and are extremely fragrant to spark your cravings. The crunch of almonds makes it a perfect delicacy.

Serves: 4

Ingredients

- A tablespoon of oil
- 100g of couscous
- 50g of flaked almonds
- 400g of chopped tomatoes
- 2 onions
- 1.5 teaspoons of cinnamon
- A garlic clove
- A tablespoon of honey
- A large handful of coriander
- 2.5 cm piece of ginger

- A teaspoon of cumin
- 50g coriander
- 250ml chicken stock
- 100g of dried apricots
- 500g of skinless chicken thigh fillets

Directions

- Take a large pan of heat oil and fry onions for about 8 minutes
- Toss in spices, garlic, and ginger to cook for another 2 minutes
- Place chicken fillets in the pan
- Fry until they are brown in about 5 minutes
- Add stock, honey, tomatoes, and apricots to boil
- Let the water bubble and then cover the pan to cook for 30 minutes
- Stir in the couscous
- Allow it to simmer for another 6 minutes
- Sprinkle coriander and almonds and serve with yogurt

Quick Moroccan Couscous

The name says it all. This recipe is specifically for those who love couscous and have a profound craving for Moroccan cuisine but do not have enough time to prepare couscous. It greatly reduces the time but offers an incredible taste.

Servings: 6

Ingredients

- Half a cup golden raisins
- A shallot
- 3 tablespoons of lemon juice
- A tablespoon of butter
- Half a cup silvered almonds
- 2 cups water
- 6 garlic cloves
- Half a cup kosher salt
- A tablespoon of olive oil
- Half a cup yellow onion
- $1/4^{th}$ of a teaspoon black pepper
- Half a cup sun-dried tomatoes
- A cup of couscous

Directions

- Take a saucepan to boil water
- Stir in couscous and cook for 15 minutes
- Use a skillet to heat olive oil
- Toss in garlic, onion, and shallot to cook until brown

- Stir dried tomatoes, almonds, raisins and onion into a mixture
- Cook and stir it for about 5 minutes
- Use pepper and salt to season couscous
- Drizzle lemon juice
- Take skillet off the heat and add butter to couscous

Moroccan Spiced Vegetable Couscous

Do you and your friends like spices? Moroccan spices in particular? Well, if yes, then here comes a great recipe for you. Just call on your friends and give them a buzz of North African spices. Everyone would love it.

Serves: 4

Ingredients

- 2 tablespoons of olive oil
- Half a teaspoon paprika
- A medium red onion
- A sweet yellow pepper
- 2 garlic cloves
- Half a teaspoon ground cumin
- 14 ounces of drained chickpeas
- A chopped carrot
- 300ml chicken vegetable stock
- Half a teaspoon of coriander
- One-fourth of a teaspoon salt
- Half a teaspoon celery salt
- Handful of chopped parsley

- Cinnamon (1/8 teaspoon)
- Cayenne pepper (1/4 teaspoon, optional)
- A cup of couscous
- ¼ teaspoon turmeric
- A cup of frozen peas
- 6 PeppadewPiquante pepper

Directions

- Take a medium skillet to heat oil
- Toss in yellow pepper, red onion, and carrot
- Cook for 10 minutes
- Make sure that the veggies are tender
- Add garlic before cooking for another minute
- Take skillet off the heat
- Use a saucepan to boil stock
- Toss in peas to cook for a minute
- Now mix all the remaining ingredients to stir
- Cover them and remove from heat for 5 minutes
- Fluff with a fork after drizzling vegetable mixture

Moroccan Chicken With Buttered Couscous

The soothing fragrance of butter on chicken couscous. Yes, that is exactly what your buds need right now. What are you waiting for? Get your hands on this recipe and enjoy a perfect flavorsome combination.

Servings: 2

Ingredients

- A tablespoon of butter
- A teaspoon of ground cumin
- Half a teaspoon paprika and cinnamon, each
- A tablespoon of oil
- 1/3 cup of blanched almonds
- 2 chicken wings (roasted)
- A small red onion
- Half a cup chicken drumsticks
- 3.5 tablespoons butter
- 5.35 ounces of couscous
- A teaspoon of coriander
- Buttered couscous
- Half a cup chicken stock
- 2 tablespoons of cilantro leaves
- 1.5 ounces green olives
- 2 teaspoons of lemon rind

Directions

- Use a big pan to heat 2 teaspoons oil and butter

- Toss in almonds to toast until browned; keep them aside
- Pour in remaining oil
- Add onion and spices to cook
- Now place roasted chicken and drumsticks to coat in the mixture
- Add stock and cook for about 5 minutes
- To prepare buttered couscous, add half a cup water, stock, 1.5 tablespoons butter and leave for boiling
- Pour it over the couscous an leave for 5 minutes
- Fluff couscous with a fork
- Now sprinkle lemon, almonds, and olives over the chicken mixture
- Use butter couscous to serve with
- Garnish your dish with cilantro

Spiced Lamb Chops With Couscous

Foodies love lamb. If you are a foodie, you are definitely going to love this recipe where couscous hugs the lamb chops under its fluffy dome.

Serves: 8

Ingredients

- 1.5 cups couscous
- 3 tablespoons of olive oil
- 1.5 tablespoon of coriander
- 1.5 tablespoon of cumin
- Pepper
- Salt
- A tablespoon of unsalted butter
- 1.5 tablespoon of cinnamon
- A teaspoon of ground cloves
- 16 loin lamb chops

Directions

- Take a small bowl to combine cloves, coriander, cumin, 2 teaspoons salt, cinnamon, and pepper

- Use this spice mixture to coat the lamb
- Take 2 large skillets to heat 1.5 tablespoons of olive oil in each
- Place half lamb chops in each of them
- Brown them for 4 minutes on high heat
- Transfer to a baking sheet
- Heat the oven to 400 degrees
- Use a saucepan to boil 3 cups of water with half a teaspoon salt in it
- Before removing from heat, stir in the couscous
- Cover and leave for 5 minutes
- Bake the lamb for 10 minutes
- Fluff the couscous with fork
- Divide equally and drizzle pan juices

Moroccan-Style Chickpea Stew

Garnish the final product with chopped cilantro and instead of brown rice, serve it with whole wheat couscous. For making it spicier, season with jalapenos.

Serves: 4

Ingredients

- A handful of almonds
- Cooked couscous
- A medium potato
- 4 shallots
- 2 tablespoons of oil
- Black pepper
- A tablespoon of tomato paste
- 3 teaspoons of baharat spice
- 5 cups of tomatoes
- 3 garlic cloves
- Half a teaspoon sweet paprika
- 2 teaspoons of brown sugar
- 10 Kalamata olives
- 2 cups of chickpeas (cooked)
- ¾ teaspoon of salt
- Half a teaspoon of cayenne pepper
- 2 tablespoons of barberries (dried)
- Fresh parsley

Directions

- Chop almonds and fry in a small saucepan to dry roast
- Take a big frying pan to heat oil
- Toss in the shallots and fry until their color is glassy
- Throw in some garlic and stir until onion becomes translucent
- Throw all ground spices into the mixture of garlic and fried shallots
- Fry for roughly 2 minutes
- Add some tomato paste to the pan and stir it in the mixture
- Toss in potato, salt, sugar (half) and tomatoes
- Cover and allow it to simmer for 12 minutes
- Stir the sauce a couple of times
- Season the sauce with black pepper
- Stir in chickpeas, currants, and olives to let them warm
- Serve with couscous
- Top with parsley and almonds prepared in the first step

Aromatic Moroccan Couscous Recipe

The whole purpose of this recipe is to make you go hungry with the fragrance and then calm down your 'uncontrolled' craving with a flavorsome taste.

Serves: 6

Ingredients

- 300g of couscous
- A tablespoon of ground cumin
- 50g of pine nuts
- A garlic clove
- 4 spring onions
- A tablespoon of ground ginger, ground coriander, paprika, each
- 215g of chickpeas
- 2 tablespoons of olive oil
- 500g of mixed vegetables
- 150g of dried apricots (chopped)
- 50g of pumpkin seeds
- A vegetable stock (reduced-salt)

Directions

- Dry fry pine nuts pumpkin seeds on medium heat
- Take a pan of water and boil mixed veggies for about 4 minutes
- Add the can of chickpeas and let it boil for another minute. Drain and keep aside
- Take the pan and heat 2 tablespoons of olive oil
- Toss in 4 spring onions and a garlic clove for 2 minutes
- Stir in all the ground spices along with couscous and paprika
- Add about 425ml of boiling water and then crumble the stock cube in it
- Add cooked chickpeas and vegetables to the pan
- Toss in dry apricots; cover the lid an leave for about 5 minutes
- Fluff up the couscous with fork
- Heat for a minute
- Sprinkle the seeds and pine nuts to serve

Breakfast

Get the perfect start to the day with this healthy, high protein breakfast of couscous. Surprise your family with a new hot breakfast cereal.

Honeyed Couscous Pudding

Fans of rice pudding should try this version that uses couscous and pitted dates instead of rice and raisins. It's sweetened with honey and topped with pistachios.

Ingredients

This quick take on rice pudding is flavored with honey and orange zest. Dates had a rich, sweet flavor.

- ¾ cup chopped pitted dates
- 3 cups low-fat milk
- ¼ cup honey
- 1 cinnamon stick
- 1 teaspoon freshly grated orange zest
- 1 cup plain or whole-wheat couscous

☐ 1 teaspoon vanilla extractGround cinnamon for dusting pudding

☐ 2 tablespoons chopped skinned pistachios, (optional)

Preparation

1. Put dates in a small bowl. Add boiling water to cover. Cover the bowl and set aside.

2. Heat milk, honey, cinnamon stick and orange zest in a saucepan over medium-high heat until nearly simmering. Stir in couscous and vanilla, remove from the heat and cover. Let stand until most of the milk has been absorbed, about 20 minutes. Remove the cinnamon stick.

3. Drain the dates and stir them into the couscous. To serve, spoon into bowls and sprinkle with ground cinnamon and pistachios, if using.

4. Variation: Instead of oatmeal for breakfast, make Honeyed Couscous Pudding with half the honey. Garnish with some nonfat yogurt or a spoonful of orange marmalade.

Breakfast Couscous With Dried Fruit Compote

Start your day with couscous prepared like oatmeal and topped with compote that uses dried fruits and black tea.

Ingredients

For compote:

☐ 1 1/4 cups water
☐ 3 tablespoons packed dark brown sugar
☐ 1 1/2 cups mixed dried fruit such as apricots, cherries, cranberries, and apples, chopped if large
☐ 1 tea bag of black tea such as orange pekoe or English breakfast
☐ 1 to 3 teaspoons fresh lemon juice

For couscous:

☐ 1 cup couscous
☐ 3 tablespoons unsalted butter

- ☐ 1 1/2 cups boiling water
- ☐ 1/2 teaspoon cinnamon
- ☐ Accompaniments: chopped toasted almonds; warm milk for drizzling

Instructions

1. Make compote: Simmer water, sugar, and fruit in a small saucepan over medium heat, uncovered, stirring occasionally, until liquid just starts to become syrupy, about 8 minutes. Add tea bag and let steep off heat while making couscous.

2. Make couscous: Cook couscous in butter in a heavy medium saucepan over medium-high heat, stirring, until pale golden, about 2 minutes. Off heat, stir in water, cinnamon, and 1/8 teaspoon salt. Cover tightly. Let stand 5 minutes, then fluff.

3. To serve: Squeeze tea bag and discard, then add lemon juice to compote. Serve couscous in bowls, topped with compote.

Couscous Muffins Recipe

Have you ever considered putting chili powder, cheese and caramelized onions in a muffin? Why not? If you're making a savory muffin with couscous, those ingredients make perfect sense.

Ingredients:

- Couscous – 60 gms
- Water – 75ml (1/2 teacup)
- All purpose flour – 50 gms
- Baking powder – 1/2 tsp
- Red chilli powder – 1/4 tsp
- Black pepper powder – 1/4 tsp
- Egg – 1

- Oil – 3 tbsp
- Milk – 1/4 cup
- Cheese, grated – 3 tbsp

- ☐ Coriander leaves, chopped – 4 tbsp
- ☐ Caramelized Onions – 2 tbsp
- ☐ Salt – to taste

Instructions

1. Bring water to a bubbling boil and salt it. Pour this over the couscous. Stir it vigorously and let it be for 4 minutes. All the water will be absorbed and the couscous is ready to use. Keep it aside.

2. Sift together all purpose flour, baking powder and to this add red chilli powder, pepper powder, pinch of salt, caramelized onions, grated cheese, chopped coriander leaves and toss well. Now add the cooked couscous, give it a mix and keep aside.

3. Beat together egg, milk and oil. Pour this mixture into the dry ingredients and mix till both the wet and dry ingredients are mixed well. Do not over do it.

4. Preheat the oven at 200 Degrees Celsius (400 F).

5. Grease a muffin pan and fill the cups till 3/4th and bake for 20 minutes or till a skewer inserted comes out clean.

6. Serve hot with some tomato ketchup drizzled over.

Notes:

1. These muffins do not rise that much when compared to the others.
2. You can omit red chilli powder, cheese and caramelized onions if you do not like.
3. The salt is added in 2 parts. One to cook the couscous and second with the flour. So check the salt.
4. Oven timings will change accordingly.

Couscous Fritters With Feta

Savory ingredients like tomatoes, spring (green) onions and feta cheese are combined with couscous, formed into patties, then fried until golden.

Ingredients

☐ 175g couscous
☐ 200ml hot vegetable stock
☐ 1 egg, beaten
☐ 3 tbsp natural yogurt
☐ 85g feta cheese, cut into 1cm cubes
☐ 50g SunBlush tomato, finely chopped
☐ 3 spring onion, finely chopped
☐ 2 tbsp sunflower oil or vegetable oil

Method

1. Measure the couscous into a large heatproof bowl, pour over the hot stock, then cover with cling film. Leave to stand

for 5 mins or until the couscous has absorbed the stock and is soft. Add the egg and yogurt and mix well. Season, then fold through the cheese, tomatoes and spring onions.

2. Divide the mixture into 4 and shape into burgers. Heat the oil in a non-stick frying pan, then cook the fritters over a medium heat for 3 mins on each side until golden. Serve with a green salad and a spoonful of your favourite chutney.

Main Course

Couscous is originally a Berber dish and for this reason couscous is a speciality in many North African countries. In Morocco, we have different types and versions of couscous but if you mention "couscous" in Morocco, people will usually assume that you are referring to the most basic version of the famous dish: the 7 vegetables couscous.

Moroccan Couscous With Seven Vegetables

The 7 vegetables couscous is composed of semolina grains (granules of durum wheat), topped with vegetables and meat cooked in a super tasty and comforting broth.

Ingredients
☐1 large onion chopped (200gr)
☐600 gr slow braising beef or lamb, trimmed of excess fat. (i.e. lamb shoulder, cracked lamb shank, lamb or beef neck, beef shin). If your meat is on the bone, take into account the weight of the bone and make sure you get about 125 gr of meat per person.
☐2 tablespoons olive oil
☐ 250 gr canned chickpeas in water (or 125 gr dried chickpeas soaked in cold water overnight), drained.
☐1 tablespoon salt
☐1 teaspoon ground turmeric
☐1 teaspoon ground ginger
☐½ teaspoon ground black pepper

- ☐ Generous pinch of saffron
- ☐ 1 coriander bouquet, tied
- ☐ 2 ripe tomatoes, seeded and chopped in 2 cm large pieces
- ☐ 1 small cabbage (600gr), quartered through the base
- ☐ 1 large sweet potato (250 gr), peeled and cut into large chunks
- ☐ 300 gr turnip, peeled and cut into 3 cm lengths
- ☐ 3 carrots (300 gr), scraped and cut into 4 cm lengths
- ☐ 200 gr courgettes cut into 5 cm lengths (not necessary for baby courgettes)
- ☐ 300 gr butternut squash or pumpkin, seeded if necessary and cut into large chunks
- ☐ 4 cups dried couscous (650 gr)

Method

1. In a large casserole (minimum 5 litres capacity), heat oil over medium high heat and place the onions, the n spices, salt, pepper and half of the tomatoes pieces. meat occasionally until lightly browned, about 10 min.

2. Add 1.5 litres of water and the chickpeas. Bring to reduce to medium low heat and place the coriander bc the casserole. Cover with a lid and let gently simmer for

3. Prepare the vegetables and set aside.

4. Now is a good time to start preparing the raisins couscous. The raisin recipe is below and the plain recipe is here. The raisins are optional but if you like s

savoury dishes, you will love this addition.

5. Carefully discard the coriander bouquet and place the cabbage, turnip and carrots in the broth, cover the casserole with a lid and let it simmer for 35 min. Make sure the vegetables don't stay at the surface and are well inserted in the broth, otherwise they might not cook evenly.

6. Add the potatoes to the broth and cover the casserole for another 20 minutes.

7. Meanwhile, place some of the broth (only the liquid, about 6 tablespoons) in a separate casserole or large deep skillet, over medium heat and place the courgettes and butternut pieces. Cover with a lid and cook for 20 minutes. Flip the courgettes and butternut halfway through cooking. The reason why we cook the courgettes and the butternut separately is because once cooked, they become very fragile and they might break if you cook them in the broth with the rest of the vegetables.

8. At this stage, your broth and vegetables are ready to be served. Adjust the seasoning by adding salt if necessary.

9. Using tongs, carefully remove the meat from the casserole and cut the meat into smaller individual pieces. To serve, place warm couscous grains in a plate and top with meat, vegetables and some tablespoons of the broth to make it moist. Add raisins (optional).

Notes

1. As you can see, I used a regular casserole for this recipe as opposed to a couscousiere. In my opinion it saves a lot of time and hassle to cook the broth and the couscous grain separately and there isn't much difference in the taste. Also, I assume that the majority if you don't own a couscousiere, it will be too bad not to enjoy Moroccan couscous because of that.

2. Keep the meat in large pieces when you place it in the casserole in the beginning of the recipe. Small pieces of meat will get even smaller after hours of slow cooking and you might struggle to find them in the broth once they are cooked. In my opinion, it's simpler to cook large pieces of meat and cut them in individual pieces before serving.

3. In Morocco, people traditionally season the couscous grains with "smen" when preparing them. Smen is a type of salted fermented butter and has a very distinctive taste. If you like it, use smen instead of olive oil when preparing the couscous grains.

4. Feel free to play around with the recipe and add or use different vegetables. Moroccans traditionally use 7 vegetables because "7" is a lucky number in the Moroccan culture.

5. Make sure to insert the vegetables at the right time so the meat and the vegetables will be ready at the same time. The way I calculate the cooking time for the vegetable is very simple. I assume that the meat will take about 2 hours to cook (or more for some cuts). I leave the meat to cook in the broth (with the chickpeas, onions, tomatoes…) until it is time to insert the vegetables so they will be ready at the same time as the meat. Keep in my mind that some vegetables cook faster than others.

6. Use quinoa instead of couscous grains for a gluten free version of the 7 vegetables couscous. If you are on a vegetarian diet, omit the meat. If you like, spicy like me, add a teaspoon of harissa to your plate.

7. You can keep the couscous grains, the broth, the meat, the vegetables and the raisins for up to 3 days in the fridge.

Chorizo Beef And Couscous Stuffed Peppers

Couscous makes a great stuffing mix for all sorts of vegetables like zucchini or peppers. In this recipe, it's mixed with onions, carrots, garlic and chorizo, stuffed inside red bell peppers and cooked in a smoky sauce.

Ingredients:
- 6 long red peppers or red bell peppers
- ¼ cup couscous
- ¼ cup boiling water
- 2 tablespoons olive oil
- 1 onion, finely chopped
- 1 carrot, grated
- 2 cloves garlic, crushed
- 1 teaspoon smoked paprika
- 1 chorizo sausage, finely chopped
- ¼ cup chopped flat-leaf parsley

- ☐ 400g beef mince
- ☐ salt and freshly ground black pepper

Sauce:
- ☐ 1 tablespoon olive oil
- ☐ 1 onion, finely chopped
- ☐ 2 cloves garlic, crushed and finely chopped
- ☐ ½ teaspoon smoked paprika
- ☐ 1 400g-can chopped tomatoes
- ☐ handful fresh basil leaves

Instructions:

1. Preheat the oven to 180°C/350°F.

2. Sauce: Heat the olive oil in a saucepan and cook the onion, garlic and paprika until the onion is tender. Stir in the tomatoes, season with salt and pepper and cook over medium heat, stirring occasionally, for about 10 minutes. Add the basil, stir to combine, cover and remove from the heat. Set aside.

3. Peppers: Combine the couscous and water in a small bowl, cover and leave for 10 minutes

4. Trim the stems off the peppers and remove the seeds, keeping the peppers whole. Place in large heatproof dish and pour over enough boiling water to cover. Leave for 5 minutes then lift out and drain well. Heat the olive oil in a sauté pan and cook the onion, carrot, garlic and paprika until the onion is tender. Stir in the chorizo and parsley and cook for 1 minute. Tip

into a large bowl and cool. Add the couscous and mince, season generously and combine well.

5. To assemble: Holding each pepper upright, drop in small pieces of the stuffing then use the handle of a wooden spoon to gently push it right to the bottom of the pepper. Continue until full to the top and repeat with the remaining peppers. You may not use all of the filling. Tip the tomato sauce into a large shallow baking dish and place the peppers and their stems, on top (I secured the tops with toothpicks before baking the peppers). Roll any unused filling into balls and place around the peppers. Drizzle with a little olive oil. Cover tightly with foil and bake for 40 minutes. Uncover and bake for a further 10 minutes until golden and the peppers are tender when pierced with a skewer.

Couscous Flat Breads

Couscous used along with flour will give flatbread a distinct flavor. The finished flatbreads can be topped with a variety of vegetables and cheeses to be cooked like a pizza.

Ingredients

☐ 240g plain flour
☐ 140g couscous, pre-soaked in enough water to cover it
☐ 2 teaspoons salt
☐ 4 teaspoons sugar
☐ 10g instant yeast
☐ 1 tablespoon olive oil or sunflower oil
☐ 400ml lukewarm water

Method

1. Place all the dry ingredients into a bowl and make a well in the centre, add the oil and three quarters of the water and mix it in and mix to a soft dough, add a little more water if need be, if it is too wet add a small

amount of flour. Knead the dough for about 15 minutes, until it is smooth and elastic to the touch.

2. Place the dough back into the bowl and oil the top, cover with a clean cloth and place it in a warm place to rise to twice it's size. Pre-heat the oven to 180°C, divide the dough into 12 balls. Roll 6 of the balls out into rounds the size of a side plate. Roll the other 6 balls into sausages and place along the edge of the side-plate sized rounds to create a rim. Allow to rise to twice its size and bake for 15-20 minutes until golden brown and cooked.

Ginger Soy Israeli Couscous With Baby Bok Choy

Israeli couscous meats Asian flavor in this recipe that creates a savory, rich broth reminiscent of store-bought Ramen, but with ingredients that aren't nearly as scary as those is in the mystery packet of Ramen flavoring.

Ingredients

- 4 cups chicken stock
- 1 1/2 cups Israeli couscous
- 2 cloves garlic minced
- 1/4 cup pickled ginger coarsely chopped
- 4 heads baby bok choy cleaned and sliced crosswise into 1/2-inch ribbons
- 2 tablespoons soy sauce
- 2 tablespoons toasted sesame oil
- 1/2 teaspoon sriracha sauce or more
- 2 tablespoons chopped Tamari roasted almonds

Instructions

1. In a medium saucepan, combine chicken stock and Israeli couscous; bring to boil. Reduce heat and simmer, stirring occasionally for 8 minutes.

2. Add garlic, pickled ginger and baby bok choy. Cook and stir 2 minutes more, until vegetables and Israeli couscous are tender.

3. Remove from heat and stir in soy sauce, sesame oil, and sriracha (adding more of any one of these to taste).

4. Divide soup among 4 bowls and sprinkle with chopped almonds. Serve.

Salad

Two easy couscous salad recipe is really quick and simple to make. Those tasty couscous salad is a colourful addition to the dinner table.

Mediterranean Couscous Salad

Quick-cooking couscous lends to the 20-minute prep time of this Greek-style salad.

Ingredients

☐ 1 cup Progresso™ chicken broth (from 32-oz carton)
☐ 3/4 cup uncooked couscous
☐ 1 cup cubed plum (Roma) tomatoes (3 medium)
☐ 1 cup cubed unpeeled cucumber (1 small)
☐ 1/2 cup halved pitted kalamata olives
☐ 1/4 cup chopped green onions (about 4 medium)
☐ 1/4 cup chopped fresh or 1 tablespoon dried dill weed
☐ 2 tablespoons lemon juice
☐ 2 tablespoons olive or vegetable oil
☐ 1/8 teaspoon salt
☐ 2 tablespoons crumbled feta cheese

Directions

1. In 2-quart saucepan, heat broth to boiling. Stir in

couscous; remove from heat. Cover; let stand 5 minutes.

2. In large bowl, place tomatoes, cucumber, olives, onions and dill weed. Stir in couscous.

3. In small bowl, beat lemon juice, oil and salt with wire whisk until well blended; pour over vegetable mixture and toss. Cover; refrigerate 1 hour to blend flavors.

4. Just before serving, sprinkle with cheese.

Couscous Salad

A super speedy, healthy salad that's perfect for week nights.

Ingredients

☐ 200g (6½oz) quick-cook (instant) couscous
☐ 250ml (8fl oz) boiling water or stock
☐ 150g (5oz) cherry tomatoes, halved
☐ 1 small cucumber diced
☐ 1 red pepper, diced
☐ A handful of sultanas
☐ 1 small red onion, finely sliced
☐ 5tbsp balsamic vinegar
☐ Coriander leaves, to serve

Method

1. Place the couscous in a large bowl and pour over

the boiling water or stock. Cover the bowl with clingfilm and set aside for 5 minutes, or until the water is absorbed, then fluff with a fork.

2. Stir the cherry tomatoes, cucumber, pepper, sultanas and red onion into the couscous.

3. Make a dressing by placing the oil and balsamic vinegar in a screw-topped jar and shaking well until combined.

4. Season the couscous well with salt and freshly ground black pepper and drizzle over some of the dressing.

Part 2

Introduction

Couscous is the most famous traditional dish in the Maghreb, steamed semolina grains generally accompanied by meats (lamb, chicken ...) and various vegetables.

Tfaya couscous is the sweet and savory version of couscous, prepared with candied onions and spicy chicken ...

Couscous is from Moroccan origins. Moroccan housewives prepare couscous with meat succulent of which they only have the secret.

The couscous at fish is typically from the Essaouira region.

As for the real chicken couscous, entirely made with poultry, it is the finest couscous, a real treat for the most demanding gourmets.

A couscoussier is essential to make the couscous. It comprises a pot on which the "" fits, colander whose holes let pass the vapor which swells the semolina grains. If these two utensils do not fit together tightly and the steam tends to escape, take a strip of cotton cloth five centimeters wide, the circumference of the pot; wet it and lay it all around the edge, then adapt the "Kesskass".

A bowl can replace the "Gassa", a large bowl in which the grains is rolled. As for the "Gharbal", a special sieve which is used to standardize the grain.

It's easier now to do it with couscous prefab which is sold in most grocery stores.

To give the-couscous a more authentic taste, just put on the grain a piece of "Smén", the aged salted butter, you have to add it when you remove it from the Kesskass after the second cooking and mix it well with a wooden spoon. The grains of couscous is always served with its sweet or savory sauce depending on taste.

Tfaya, a kind of jam, is an original dish that only takes on its value when accompanied by the grains of couscous.

Generally, Moroccans eat the couscous with the fingers. They form small dumplings with seeds, vegetables, and meat of couscous.

Meat And Seven Vegetable Couscous

- **Preparation**: 45min
- **Cooking**: 1h15min
- **Difficulty**: easy
- **Price**: not expensive

Ingredients (for 8 people)

- 700g couscous semolina (fine grains)
- 100 g fresh butter

For the couscous broth:
- 1.5 kg sliced lamb collar
- 4 tbsps. Olive oil.
- 2 onions cut into thin wedges
- 500g crushed tomatoes 1 small green cabbage
- 6 crushed garlic cloves + harissa (spicy sauce) for serving.
- 1 tbsp. paprika + 1 small cinnamon stick
- 1 pinch of saffron filaments
- 500g pumpkin cut into enormous cubes
- 1 tbsp. 1 teaspoon ground black pepper

- 2 carrots cut into enormous sections
- 4 turnips cut into quarters, + 4 zucchini cut into sections
- 150g of chickpeas soaked the day before

Preparation of the recipe

Heat the olive oil in the couscoussier pot. Brown the meat on all sides, then set it aside on a platter.

In the pot, fry the onions for 1 minute, then add the tomatoes, garlic, and spices. Put the meat back, cover with plenty of water, and cooke to the boil. Add the carrots, turnips, and chickpeas.

Cover and cook for 2 hours over low heat. During this time, start the moistening the couscous with a little bit of cold water.

After an hour, salt the broth and proceed to the steaming of the couscous. Half an hour before the end of cooking, add the zucchini, pumpkin, and cabbage cut into 6 pieces.

When everything is cooked, butter the couscous and present it on a dish. Meat, vegetables, broth, and salad are served separately. Accompany with a bowl of Harissa (spicy sauce). After an hour, salt the broth and proceed to the first steaming of the couscous. Half an hour before the end of cooking, add the zucchini, pumpkin and cabbage cut into 6 pieces.

When everything is cooked, butter the couscous and present it on a dish. Meat, vegetables, broth and salad are served separately. Accompany with a bowl of harissa.

Chicken Couscous, Chickpeas And Raisins

- **Preparation**: 45min
- **Cooking**: 1h00min
- **Difficulty**: easy
- **Price**: not expensive

Ingredients (for 6 persons)

- 650g medium couscous
- 100g fresh butter, 4 tbsp oil
- 1 pinch of saffron filaments
- 1 tbsp. 1 teaspoon turmeric
- 3 tbsps. Olive oil.
- 1 tbsp. salt
- For the couscous broth:
- 1/ 2 kg farm chicken cut into 8 pieces
- 1 finely chopped onion
- 200g of chickpeas soaked the day before
- 1 pinch of saffron filaments
- 4 large onions, minced, 1/2 tsp ginger

- 125g blond raisins
- 50g clarified butter, cinnamon, nuts
- salt, freshly ground pepper

Preparation of the recipe

In the couscoussier pot, bring together the chicken, chopped onion, a pinch of cinnamon, ginger, chickpeas, saffron, butter, salt, and pepper. Cover with plenty of water and cooke it to the boil. Cover and cook over low heat.

Crumble the saffron in a bowl and cover it with 3 tablespoons of boiling water. Let sit for 5 minutes, then add the turmeric, salt, and 20 cl of cold water. Mix well.

Meanwhile, spread the couscous in an enormous dish, add the oil and mix well. Add the saffron water and let stand for 10 minutes, then crumble it between your palms and with your fingertips until all lumps disappear.

In the pot, add the sliced onions and the raisins. Steam the couscous three times during the rest of the chicken cooking [1 hour total].

Butter the couscous and put it in an enormous dish. Dig the center and place the chicken, onions, raisins, and chickpeas in it. Sprinkle a little broth and serve the rest separately.

Garnish the couscous with the cinnamon powder and dried fruit of your choice (nuts).

Couscous Of Flap With Tfaya Conger

- **Preparation**: 30min
- **Cooking**: 1h00min
- **Difficulty**: easy
- **Price**: not expensive

Ingredients (for 6 persons)

- 500g couscous semolina (medium grains)
- 4 tablespoons olive oil
- 100g clarified butter
- 1 kg of conger cut into steaks
- 1 finely chopped onion + 1 bunch of chopped cilantro
- 3 tbsps. Olive oil, + salt, freshly ground pepper.
- 1 good pinch of saffron filaments
- For the tfaya:
- 4 large white onions
- 75g raisins
- 50g butter
- 1 tbsp. honey

- 1 tbsp. 1 tsp cinnamon
- 100g hulled almonds

Preparation of the recipe

In the couscoussier pot, for 1.2l of water. Add the chopped onion, olive oil, saffron, salt, and pepper. Boil the water.

Pour the couscous into a large container or a bowl, add the olive oil and mix. Pour 30 cl of cold salted water and shake the container to distribute the water well. Let swell for 15 minutes, then mill the couscous (crumble it between your palms and with your fingertips) until all lumps disappear.

Pour the couscous in the couscoussier's colander, insulate the joint with folded white paper and cook for about 20 minutes, until the steam crosses the couscous.

Put the couscous back in the dish, add 1 glass of water and milk. Steam again for 20 minutes and re-mill before a third 5-minute steam cut.

Steam the couscous with this broth in two 20-minute passes. Put the slices of conger in the pot between the two steam passages.

During this cooking, prepare the tfaya:

Cut the onions into thin rings and blanch them for 1 minute in boiling water. Melt the butter in a saucepan and brown the onions for a long time over very low heat. When they are blond and. fluffy, add the drained raisins, honey, almonds, and cinnamon. Mix well and remove from heat.

Butter the couscous, put it in an enormous dish, place the slices of conger on the couscous and sprinkle with a little broth. Surround the fish in the tfaya, sprinkle with fresh coriander, and serve the rest of the broth separately.

Lamb Couscous With Cardoons

- **Preparation**: 45min
- **Cooking**: 1h15min
- **Difficulty**: easy
- **Price**: not expensive

Ingredients(for 8 people)

- 1kg couscous semolina medium grains
- 1 bunch of kharchouf (cardoons)
- 1kg shoulder of lamb collar
- 3 chopped onions
- 2 turnips, 6 carrots, 3 zucchini
- 100g chickpeas soaked the day before
- 1/2 tsp. special couscous ras-el-hanout
- 1/2 tsp. white pepper
- 2.5 tsp. tomato puree
- 3 tsp. olive oil
- 1 tsp. salt
- 30 g butter

Preparation of the recipe

Peel, wash and cut carrots, onions, zucchini, and turnips.

Remove the leaves and the filaments from the cardoons and cut them into 5 cm sections.

In the bottom of the couscoussier, put the oil, the meat cut into pieces, 1/2 tablespoon of salt, the ras-el-hanout, onion, chili, 2 tablespoons of tomato puree, and cook it for a good 5 minutes over medium heat.

Add 2 liters of water, add the chickpeas, carrots, cardoons, and turnips and cook for 1 hour.

Steam the couscous semolina with the couscoussier for 20 min. Take out the semolina and pour it into a dish.

Repeat the milling operation between each cooking 2 times. Coat it with butter.

When the meat is cooked, add the rest of the vegetables, 1/2 teaspoon of salt, 1/2 teaspoon of tomato puree; moisten with water just above the vegetables. Cook for 30 minutes.

Make the couscous; sprinkle with the sauce and vegetables, then arrange the meat around.

Couscous With Onions, Tomatoes And Broad Beans

- **Preparation**: 15min
- **Cooking**: 30min
- **Difficulty**: easy
- **Price**: not expensive

Ingredients(for 6 persons)

- 1kg of fresh beans
- 750g couscous semolina (medium grains)
- 750g fresh tomatoes
- 500g chopped white onions
- 1/2 liter of milk
- 1 fresh green pepper
- 1/2 tsp. salt

Preparation of the recipe

Prepare couscous semolina:

Put the semolina in a large bowl, add 3 tablespoons of oil, and mix by hand until all the couscous is soaked in oil.

Boil 1.5 liters of water in the bottom of the couscoussier and fill the top with semolina. Cook until the steam escapes and add 1 liter of water, then pour the couscous back into the large bowl. Add the salt and wet the semolina with an additional 50 cl of water, then leave to swell until the water is completely absorbed.

Air and separate the couscous grains by hand, then put them back in the top of the couscous maker and cook for about 10 min until the steam escapes again.

Put the couscous back in the salad bowl with a knob of butter. Again, separate and air the couscous beans.

Prepare the couscous filling:

Remove the ends of the beans and rid them of the filaments. Cut the pods into sections (similar seeds). Wash and drain. Boil the tomatoes, peel them and puree them.

In a casserole dish, put the tomato puree, the broad beans, the onions, the salt, the split pepper in half, and 50 cl of water.

Close and cook for 15 min, add the milk, and extend for 2 min.

Make the couscous with the beans and the sauce.

Mushroom Couscous

- **Preparation**: 25min
- **Cooking**: 1h00min
- **Difficulty**: easy
- **Price**: not expensive

Ingredients(for 6 persons)

- 1.3 kg lamb collar
- 750 g couscous semolina (fine grains)
- 1 kg button mushrooms
- 5 garlic cloves
- 2 chopped onions
- 100 g chickpeas having soaked for 12 hours
- 1 tsp. coffee from ras-el-hanout
- 1 new onion
- 1 tsp, chilli
- 1 tsp. 1 teaspoon turmeric
- 2 tsp. chopped fresh cilantro
- 2 tsp. tomato puree
- 2 tsp. olive oil

Preparation of the recipe

Prepare couscous semolina:

Put the semolina in a large bowl, add 3 tablespoons of oil, and mix by hand until all the couscous is soaked in oil.

Boil 1.5 liters of water in the bottom of the couscoussier and fill the top with semolina. Cook until the steam escapes and add 1 liter of water, then pour the couscous back into the large bowl. Add the salt and wet the semolina with an additional 50 cl of water, then leave to swell until the water is completely absorbed.

separate the couscous grains by hand, then put them back in the top of the couscous maker and cook for about 10 min until the steam escapes again.

Put the couscous back in the bowl with 100g of butter. Again, separate the couscous grains. You will get a very light couscous.

Prepare the couscous broth:

In a pressure cooker, put the oil, the meat cut into pieces, 1/2 tablespoon of salt, the chili pepper, the turmeric, the ras-el-hanout*, the minced garlic, the tomato puree, and fry 5.min over medium heat. Add the chickpeas and 1.5 liters of water. Cook for 30 minutes under pressure.

Wash and cut the mushrooms in half or four pieces depending on their size. Peel, wash, and cut the carrots into sections.

Once the meat is cooked, remove it from the pressure cooker. Put the mushrooms, and two chopped onions in the sauce with 1/2 teaspoon of salt, then, if necessary, add water to the height of the vegetables and cook for 15 min under pressure. Open and add the chopped new onion. Cook 5 min without pressurizing, then add the coriander.

Dress up the couscous, sprinkle with sauce and vegetables, then arrange the meat.

Serve this Mushroom Couscous with green beans as an accompaniment.

Ras-El-Hanout: A mixture of morocan special spices .

Seafood Couscous

- **Preparation**: 20min
- **Cooking**: 45min
- **Difficulty**: easy
- **Price**: not expensive

Ingredients(for 4 people)

Couscous broth:

- 1kg seafood cocktail (shrimp, calamari, mussels)
- 2 red peppers
- 1 chopped onion
- 6 chopped garlic cloves
- 3 tsp. chopped fresh cilantro
- 1/2 tsp. coffee from ras-el-hanout
- 1 tsp. 1 tsp sweet pepper
- 2 tsp. tomato puree
- 3 tsp. olive oil
- Preparation of couscous semolina:
- 500g couscous semolina (medium grain)
- 2 tsp. vegetable oil

- 1 knob of butter, 1 tsp. 1 teaspoon fine salt

Preparation of the recipe

Prepare couscous semolina:

Put the semolina in a bowl, add 2 tablespoons of oil, and mix it by hand until all the couscous is soaked in oil.

Boil 1 liter of water at the bottom of the couscoussier and fill the top with semolina. Cook until steam escapes and add 1 liter of water, then pour the couscous back into the bowl.

Add the salt and wet the semolina with 30 cl of additional water, then leave to swell until the water is completely absorbed.

Separate the couscous grains by hand, then put them back in the top of the couscous maker and cook for about 10 min until the steam escapes again. Put the couscous back in the bowl with a knob of butter. Again, separate and air the couscous beans. You will get a very light couscous.

Seafood preparation:

In a frying pan, put the oil, the seafood, the onion, the peppers cut into strips, and sauté 10 min over low heat.

Add the salt, sweet pepper, ras-el-hanout*, chopped garlic, and the tomato puree diluted in 50 cl of water. Mix then cover and let reduce 20 min over low heat.

At the end of cooking, add the chopped cilantro. Serve the semolina with the sauce on top.

Couscous With Prunes And Lamb

- **Preparation**: 45min
- **Cooking**: 1h30min
- **Difficulty**: easy
- **Price**: not expensive

Ingredients(for 8 people)

- 1kg leg of lamb, cut into large cubes
- 1 onion + 1 spoon. 1 teaspoon turmeric
- 2 tbsp. clarified butter
- 1 tbsp. 1 teaspoon ras el-hanout
- 1 pinch of saffron filaments
- 1/2 tsp. 1 teaspoon salt, freshly ground pepper
- For couscous:
- 500g of fine couscous
- 1 cinnamon stick + 100g butter
- For garnish:
- 300g prunes, 30g blond grapes
- 1 chopped onion + 100g whole hulled almonds

- 2 tbsp. clarified butter
- 1 tbsp. honey
- 1 tbsp. ground cinnamon

Preparation of the recipe

Put prunes for 2 hours in a little lukewarm water, drain and pit them.

Pour water half way up the couscoussier pot. Heat and add the butter, lamb, chopped onion, and spices. Salt lightly (the broth should reduce). Bring to a boil, cover, and cook for 2 hours on low heat.

Once the couscous is moistened and milled, mix in the cinnamon stick broken into small pieces. start steaming after one hour of cooking the meat.

To prepare the prune filling, fry the onion in the butter for 3 minutes. Add the prunes, almonds, and raisins. Cook for 5 minutes on very low heat then, off the heat, add the honey and cinnamon.

When the couscous is cooked, remove the colander from the couscoussier and reduce the broth over high heat to concentrate it. Meanwhile, butter the couscous and spoon it into a large dish.

Place the meat and the filling in the center of the couscous and drizzle with a few ladles of broth. Serve the rest separately.

Chicken Couscous With Apples

- **Preparation**: 30min
- **Cooking**: 1h00min
- **Difficulty**: easy
- **Price**: not expensive

Ingredients(for 6 persons)

For the couscous grains:
- 700g of fine couscous semolina
- 200 g raisins
- 6 tbsp. oil soup
- 4 tbsp. acacia honey
- 25 g butter
- **Salt**
- For garnish:
- 4 chicken thighs
- 4 reinette apples + 1 spoon. liquid honey
- 1 onion + 1 spoon. 1 teaspoon turmeric
- 100 g butter + Salt, pepper
- 1 tbsp. caster sugar

- 1 tbsp. 1 tsp coriander powder
- 1 tbsp. ground cinnamon

Preparation of the recipe

Prepare the semolina:

Put the semolina in a bowl, add 2 tablespoons of oil, and mix it by hand until all the couscous is soaked in oil.

Boil 1 liter of water at the bottom of the couscoussier and fill the top with semolina. Cook until steam escapes and add 1 liter of water, then pour the couscous back into the bowl.

Add the salt and wet the semolina with 30 cl of additional water, then leave to swell until the water is completely absorbed.

Separate the couscous grains by hand, then put them back in the top of the couscous maker and cook for about 10 min until the steam escapes again. Put the couscous back in the bowl with a knob of butter. Again, separate and air the couscous beans. You will get a very light couscous.

Rinse the raisins and add them to the couscous before the second steaming. At the end of cooking, add the acacia honey to the semolina, then mix thoroughly with your hands.

Peel the onion and chop it. Heat 50 g butter in a casserole dish, add the chicken thighs and brown them. Add the onion and continue cooking over medium heat, until the onion turns brown, stirring occasionally. Season with spices, salt, sugar, then pours 1.5 l of water. Cover and simmer for 45 minutes.

Peel the apples, and cut them into strips of about 2 cm. Heat the remaining butter in a pan. Cook the apples for 10 minutes over medium heat until golden on each side. Pepper very lightly.

Serve the couscous drizzled with sauce. Decorate with chicken thighs and apples, on which you will spread the liquid honey.

Three Meat Royal Couscous

- **Preparation**: 45min
- **Cooking**: 1h00min
- **Difficulty**: easy
- **Price**: not expensive

Ingredients(for 6 persons)

For the couscous grains:
- 700 g fine couscous semolina
- 6 tbsp. oil soup
- 25 g butter
- Salt

For garnish:
- 350 g beef collar
- 350 g lamb shoulder
- 2 chicken legs, 200 g chickpeas soaked the day before
- 3 medium zucchini, 3 carrots
- 2 onions; 1/2 tsp. 1 teaspoon ground red pepper

- 3 garlic cloves, 3 tbsp. oil soup
- 1 chili, 1 tablespoon. 1 tsp black pepper
- 1 tablespoon double tomato puree
- 1 tbsp. ras el hanout
- 8 sociges

Preparation of the recipe

Prepare couscous semolina:

Put the semolina in a bowl, add 2 tablespoons of oil, and mix it by hand until all the couscous is soaked in oil.

Boil 1 liter of water at the bottom of the couscoussier and fill the top with semolina. Cook until steam escapes and add 1 liter of water, then pour the couscous back into the bowl.

Add the salt and wet the semolina with 30 cl of additional water, then leave to swell until the water is completely absorbed.

Separate the couscous grains by hand, then put them back in the top of the couscous maker and cook for about 10 min until the steam escapes again. Put the couscous back in the bowl with a knob of butter. Again, separate and air the couscous beans. You will get a very light couscous.

Peel the garlic cloves and onions; chop them. Cut the beef and lamb into pieces. Wash the zucchini and remove the ends, then cut them into quarters.

Heat the oil in a pot. Brown the pieces of meat (beef and lamb) over low heat for 3 minutes.

Add the garlic and onions, stir then add the double tomato puree. Salt and season with the spices. Moisten with 1.5 l of water, mix and simmer for 1 hour 15 minutes over medium heat.

Reduce the heat, then add the chicken thighs. Continue cooking for 10 minutes over medium heat.

Then add the zucchini, the whole pepper, and cook for 15 minutes.

Serve the couscous in a large dish. Arrange the meats, then the zucchini on the couscous. Present the sauce separately, and sprinkle before serving.

Lentil Couscous With Vegetables

- **Preparation**: 15min
- **Cooking**: 45min
- **Difficulty**: easy
- **Price**: not expensive

Ingredients(for 6 persons)

For the couscous grains:
- 600 g fine couscous semolina
- 6 tbsp. oil soup
- 25 g butter

For garnish :
- 400 g blond lentils
- 2 turnips
- 2 carrots 2 onions
- 2 cloves garlic
- 1 cube of vegetable broth
- 2 tbsp. oil soup
- 1 cooked. ground cinnamon
- Salt pepper

Preparation of the recipe

Preparation of the recipe

Peel the onions and cloves of garlic; chop them. Pour everything into a casserole dish. Add the oil, then fry over low heat for 5 minutes. Season with salt, pepper, cinnamon, and bouillon cube. Wet everything with 1L of water.

Sort and wash the Lentils with plenty of water. Peel the carrots and turnips. Cut them into sticks. Add all the vegetables to the broth. Cook for 40 minutes over medium heat.

During this time, prepare the semolina as indicated below for semolina preparation.

Place the couscous in a large deep dish. Generously sprinkle the semolina with sauce. Scatter the lentils over the couscous. Garnish with carrot sticks and turnips.

.

Cinnamon Sweet Couscous

- **Preparation**: 30min
- **Cooking**: 2h00min
- **Difficulty**: easy
- **Price**: not expensive

Ingredients(for 6 persons)

- 500 g medium couscous grains
- 200 g raisins
- 1 tablespoon ground cinnamon
- 80 g diced butter
- 80 cl of water
- 1 liter of hot tea
- 80 g icing sugar
- 10 cl of orange blossom water
- 1 liter of fermented milk (optional)
- 1/2 teaspoon of fine salt
- 2 oranges in quarters
- 150 g fried hulled almonds

Preparation of the recipe

Preparation of the recipe

Sink the raisins in hot tea. Let them swell for 1 hour. Drain and set aside.

Steam the couscous:

Put the semolina in a bowl, covered with 80 cl of well-salted and cold water, and 2 good tablespoons of oil.

Mix very quickly and let swell for about 30 min.

After this time, take a large bowl, pour the semolina and roll it between your hands for the first time. Place it in the couscoussier over boiling water.

Close well and wait 10 min, while the steam passes through the semolina.

Take the semolina, pour it into the large bowl, put 80 g of butter in small pieces, and whisk well with a fork.

Add salt, pepper, and cinnamon, mix, and let cool a little. Roll it a second time with the warm mixture.

Add the sugar, orange blossom water, three-quarters of the cinnamon and the raisins. Mix carefully, sprinkle with the rest of the cinnamon and serve immediately, decorated with oranges and almonds.

you can accompany this couscous with fermented milk.

Beef And Vegetable Couscous

- **Preparation**: 35min
- **Cooking**: 2h00min
- **Difficulty**: easy
- **Price**: not expensive

Ingredients(for 8 people)

For the couscous grains:
- 700 g fine couscous semolina
- 100g raisins
- 6 tbsp. oil soup
- 25 g butter
- **Salt**

For garnish:
- 1 kg of beef (collar or shoulder)
- 500g of pumpkin
- 6 carrots
- 350g peeled tomatoes with their juice (canned)
- 4 onions
- 250 g natural chickpeas (canned)
- 4 tbsp. oil soup

- 1 tsp. teaspoon ras and hanout, salt and pepper

Preparation of the recipe

Prepare the semolina.

Put the semolina in a bowl, add 2 tablespoons of oil, and mix it by hand until all the couscous is soaked in oil.

Boil 1 liter of water at the bottom of the couscoussier and fill the top with semolina. Cook until steam escapes and add 1 liter of water, then pour the couscous back into the bowl.

Add the salt and wet the semolina with 30 cl of additional water, then leave to swell until the water is completely absorbed.

Separate the couscous grains by hand, then put them back in the top of the couscous maker and cook for about 10 min until the steam escapes again. Put the couscous back in the bowl with a knob of butter. Again, separate and air the couscous beans. You will get a very light couscous.

After the first steaming, add the raisins to the couscous grains .

Peel the onions and chop them. Heat the oil in a pot and fry the pieces of beef. Add the onions. Salt, pepper, and spice with the Ras-El-Hanout. Add the peeled tomatoes, then simmer for 15 minutes.

Peel the pumpkin slice and remove the seeds and stringy parts. Cut the flesh into large cubes. Peel the carrots and cut them into sections.

Pour these vegetables into the pot with the chickpeas. Cover with plenty of water and cook for about 2 hours, covered, over low heat.

Present the couscous in a large dish, place the meat in the center, and the vegetables around. Serve the hot sauce separately. Sprinkle the semolina with the sauce just before serving.

Chicken Peas And Pumpkin Couscous

- **Preparation**: 45min
- **Cooking**: 1h00min
- **Difficulty**: easy
- **Price**: not expensive

Ingredients(for 8 people)

- 1 chicken 1.6 kg ready to cook
- 380g (2 cups) couscous
- 650g of pumpkin, peeled, seeded, cut into 2 cm pieces)
- 1 tablespoon olive oil
- 1 tablespoon paprika + 1 x 400g can of chickpeas, rinsed, drained
- 2 teaspoon ground cumin
- 2 teaspoon ground coriander
- 1 x 7cm cinnamon stick + 1/2 teaspoon of turmeric
- 1 piece of ground ginger + 1 pinch of saffron pistils
- 2 x 425g cans of diced tomatoes

- 1 red onion, cut in half, cut into wedges
- 1 tablespoon extra olive oil
- 250 ml (1 cup) boiling water
- 3 garlic cloves, finely chopped + 250ml chicken broth (1 cup)
- Sprigs of fresh coriander and Harissa, to serve

Preparation of the recipe

Wash the inside and outside of the chicken with cold water. Place chicken, chest down, on a clean work surface.

Use poultry shears or sharp kitchen shears to cut along each side of the spine. Discard the spine. Cut the breast in half along the breastbone. Use a sharp knife to cut around the legs, between the thigh and the chest. Cut the thigh sticks. Cut the wings and the breast and cut each breast in half diagonally. Season with salt and pepper.

Heat the oil in a large pot (bottom of the couscoussier) over medium-high heat. Add half the chicken and cook for 3 minutes on each side or until golden brown. Transfer to a large dish. Repeat with the remaining chicken.

Add the onion and garlic to the pan. Reduce heat to low and cook, stirring occasionally, for 5 minutes or until onion is tender. Add paprika, cumin, ground coriander, cinnamon, ginger, turmeric, and saffron. Cook, stirring, for 1 minute or until the aromatics mix.

Add the chicken, tomatoes, and broth. Season with salt and pepper. Cover and cook for 20 minutes.

Meanwhile, place the couscous in a large heat-resistant bowl. Add the extra oil. Add the water. Cover and let stand for 5 minutes or until the liquid is absorbed. Use a fork to separate the grains.

Add the pumpkin and chickpeas to the chicken mixture. Place the steamed couscous on the pot and cook, uncovered, for 30 minutes or until the chicken, pumpkin, and couscous are tender.

Transfer the couscous to a bowl. Stir in 3/4 cup (185ml) cooking juices from the chicken mixture. Transfer to the center of a large serving dish. Place the chicken in the couscous. Garnish with fresh cilantro. Serve with harissa.

Tfaya Couscous With Chicken And Caramelized Onions

- **Preparation**: 1h00min
- **Cooking**: 1h30min
- **Difficulty**: easy
- **Price**: not expensive

Ingredients(for 6 persons)

- 1 chicken of about 2kg
- 1kg of couscous
- 2kg of onions
- 200g raisins
- 1 liter of clear poultry stock
- 5 tablespoons of sugar
- 1 tablespoon rinsed butter
- 1 tablespoon butter
- Oil, 100g peeled and toasted almonds
- 1 cinnamon stick
- 4 cloves
- 1 teaspoon of ginger

- 1 teaspoon pepper, salt
- 1/2 teaspoon ground cinnamon
- 1 pinch of saffron, 4 hard-boiled eggs to decorate

Preparation of the recipe

Put the onions cut into strips, the cloves and the cinnamon stick in a saucepan. Moisten with a liter of water, salt. Bring to a boil.

Halfway through cooking, add the raisins, the cinnamon powder, and the butter. Cook until the water has completely evaporated, then add the sugar and caramelize the onions, stirring constantly.

In a couscous pan, put the chicken, add an onion cut into strips, two tablespoons of oil, ginger and saffron, salt, and pepper. Moisten with chicken stock and a liter of water, bring to a boil.

Prepare the couscous in a large tray, sprinkle lightly with salted cold water, and with the palms of the hands, roll the couscous by passing the hands over the grains in a regular movement.

Pour the couscous into the top of the couscoussier and place it on the boiling pan. Tie the two utensils with a strip of cloth dipped in a paste of flour and water so that the steam escapes only from the top. After the steam has escaped, cook for half an hour.

Remove the couscous, pour it into the tray, crush it, cool it, add cold water, aerate it, and sprinkle it again until the swollen grains are saturated with water. Let rest.

Repeat the previous operation with the couscous, but this time adding two tablespoons of oil.

When steam escapes from the couscous. Cook for 15 minutes, then remove and place it in a large round dish, coat with rinsed butter.

Place the chicken in the center of the plate , place the caramelized onions, sprinkle with broth and garnish with skinned and toasted almonds then the eggs cut in 2.

Serve immediately with separate broth in a bowl.

Moroccan Couscous With Nuts

- **Preparation**: 25min
- **Cooking**: 30min
- **Difficulty**: easy
- **Price**: not expensive

Ingredients(for 6 persons)

- For the couscous grains:
- 600 g fine couscous semolina
- 6 tbsp. oil soup
- 100 g butter
- For garnish:
- 250 g hulled almonds
- 100 g hazelnuts
- 100 g cashews
- 100 g walnut kernels
- 100g pistachios
- 5 tbsp. powdered cane sugar
- 2 sachets of vanilla sugar

Preparation of the recipe

In a large bowl, pour water over the couscous until it is just wet. Let sit for 10 minutes. In the meantime heat water in the lower part of the couscoussier.

Then stir the grains between the fingers so that they all come off from each other. Then place them in the upper part of the couscoussier and cook for 15 minutes. (The cooking time depends on the couscous on your tast).

Pour the almonds and cashews in a dish and lightly brown them in the oven on low heat.

Finely chop 150 g of golden baked, then add them to the couscous. Then add the sugars, hazelnuts, and whole pistachios.

Place the couscous in a large hollow dish, place some dried fruit in the center, then draw a star with the walnut kernels. Decorate the outline of the dish with the remaining nuts.

Dried Fruit Couscous

- **Preparation**: 25min
- **Cooking**: 30min
- **Difficulty**: easy
- **Price**: not expensive

Ingredients(for 6 persons)

- For the couscous grains:
- 600 g medium couscous semolina
- 100g raisins
- 6 tablespoon of oil
- 100g butter
- For garnish:
- 1 orange
- 100 g dried apricots
- 100 g Agen prunes
- 100 g dates
- 3 tbsp. sugar

Preparation of the recipe

Prepare the semolina.

Put the semolina in a bowl, add 2 tablespoons of oil, and mix it by hand until all the couscous is soaked in oil.

Boil 1 liter of water at the bottom of the couscoussier and fill the top with semolina. Cook until steam escapes and add 1 liter of water, then pour the couscous back into the bowl.

Add the salt and wet the semolina with 30 cl of additional water, then leave to swell until the water is completely absorbed.

Separate the couscous grains by hand, then put them back in the top of the couscous maker and cook for about 10 min until the steam escapes again. Put the couscous back in the bowl with a knob of butter. Again, separate and air the couscous beans. You will get a very light couscous..

Squeeze the orange and add the sugar to the juice. Drizzle the couscous with sweet orange juice. Gently mix with your hands.

Remove the pits from prunes and dates. Cut them into small pieces, adding the apricots. Steam the dried fruit for 20 minutes.

Present the couscous in a round dish. Decorate the dish by placing the dried fruit over the entire surface of the couscous.

This dish is traditionally served to diners as a second meal, after having served a meat tagine or a chicken tagine.

Serve this dried fruit couscous with whole milk yogurt as a dessert, or serve it with duck breast with honey to make it a main dish.

Roasted Lamb Couscous

- **Preparation**: 45min
- **Cooking**: 1h30min
- **Difficulty**: easy
- **Price**: not expensive

Ingredients(for 8 people)

- For the couscous grains:
- 800 g fine couscous semolina
- 6 tbsp. oil soup
- 25 g butter, Salt
- For garnish:
- 1 1.5 kg roast lamb (saddle and leg of lamb)
- 4 garlic cloves
- 4 medium carrots
- 4 tbsp. olive oil
- 1 sprig of thyme
- 1 tbsp. 1 teaspoon ras el hanout
- salt and freshly ground black pepper

Preparation of the recipe

This recipe of roasted lamb couscous is ideal for meals with friends. Lamb, a highly prized meat, brings flavor and a friendly touch, especially for outdoor meals.

Prepare the semolina.

Put the semolina in a bowl, add 2 tablespoons of oil, and mix it by hand until all the couscous is soaked in oil.

Boil 1 liter of water at the bottom of the couscoussier and fill the top with semolina. Cook until steam escapes and add 1 liter of water, then pour the couscous back into the bowl.

Add the salt and wet the semolina with 30 cl of additional water, then leave to swell until the water is completely absorbed.

Separate the couscous grains by hand, then put them back in the top of the couscous maker and cook for about 10 min until the steam escapes again. Put the couscous back in the bowl with a knob of butter. Again, separate and air the couscous beans. You will get a very light couscous.

Pour the olive oil in a bowl in which you crumble the sprig of thyme. Preheat the oven to 240 ° C.

Scrape the carrots and cut them into rings. Peel the cloves of garlic, cut them in half lengthwise to remove the germ, then cut them in half. Make incisions in the skin of the roast and push in the garlic pieces.

Pour three bowls of water into a pot, stir in the Ras-El-Hanout, pepper, and salt. Add the carrots, then the leg, cook for 20 minutes, covered, over medium heat.

Carefully remove the leg. Continue cooking the vegetables for another 10 minutes. Brush the roast with thyme-flavored oil and place it in a dish. Bake the meat for 30 minutes, basting it occasionally with the cooking juices.

Present the couscous in a large dish. Garnish with carrots. Cut the roast lamb in a nice serving dish, Serve the sauce and the meat separately.

Delicious Couscous Recipes

Recipe 1: Garlic Shrimp And Couscous

Shrimp and garlic go together. Couscous and garlic do get along well together also. I hope that you appreciate this very last dish of our couscous cookbook. We think it's a great one to prepare on a weekend night, and possibly pour yourself a nice glass of your favorite wine. Enjoy!

List of Ingredients:

- 1 pound uncooked, peeled, and deveined medium shrimp
- 4 cups cooked couscous
- ¼ cups marinated roasted peppers
- 2 minced cloves garlic
- ½ cup diced red onion
- 2 Tablespoons unsalted butter
- 2 Tablespoons fresh chopped parsley

- 2 Tablespoons fresh chopped cilantro
- 2 tablespoons lemon juice
- **1 tablespoon lemon zest**

Yield: 4
Cooking Time: **30 minutes**

Instructions:

You will work on preparing the shrimp first and simply keep the couscous warm until ready.

In a large skillet, heat the butter and cook the garlic and onion for 5-6 minutes.

Add the shrimp and the herbs, roasted peppers, lemon juice, and lemon zest.

Continue cooking until the shrimp are done, or pink.

Once the shrimp are cooked, serve them on a bed of warm couscous and enjoy fully.

Recipe 2: Roasted Pumpkin Couscous Dish

I always try to find new recipes to use up my pumpkin leftovers after Halloween. Add some nuts and maybe a few green veggies and you have a beautiful and very yummy dish to enjoy with friends and family.

List of Ingredients:

- 2 cups fresh cubed pumpkin
- 2 Tablespoons sesame seeds
- 2 Tablespoons sesame oil
- 3 cups cooked couscous
- 2 cups chopped kale leaves
- ½ cup roasted chopped cashews
- 1 tablespoon lemon juice
- 1 tablespoon orange juice
- Pinch garlic powder
- **Salt, black pepper**

Yield: 4
Cooking Time: **40 minutes**

Instructions:

In a large skillet, heat the sesame oil.

Sauté the cubed pumpkin in sesame oil, with the sesame seeds, lemon juice, and orange juice.

After 10 minutes, add the kale, and then finally the couscous and the rest of the ingredients.

Serve warm and adjust the seasonings for sure before serving.

Recipe 3: Couscous Cakes For Everyone

You can serve these cakes and people might think you are serving them some fancy crab cakes. Make sure you serve with your favorite dipping sauce and perhaps lime or lemon wedges, for sure.

List of Ingredients:

- 4 cups of cooked couscous (your very favorite brand)
- 4 large eggs
- ½ chopped medium yellow onion
- Pinch red pepper flakes
- Pinch nutmeg
- Salt, black pepper
- 1 tablespoon lime zest
- 1 tablespoon lime juice
- Olive oil for cooking
- ½ cup shredded mozzarella cheese
- ½ tsp baking powder
- 3 Tablespoons all-purpose flour
- **3 Tablespoons cooking oil or butter, your choice**

Yield: 4
Cooking Time: **30 minutes**

Instructions:

In a large mixing bowl, add the cooked couscous, onion, all seasonings, lime juice, lime zest, mozzarella cheese, baking powder, and flour.

In a second bowl, whisk the eggs together.

Add the eggs to the first mixture and form the patties or cakes.

Heat the butter or oil, your preference, and cook the cakes for about 5 minutes on each side or until they are just golden enough to be eaten.

Enjoy with a dipping sauce, such as ranch or spicy mayonnaise.

Recipe 4: Fried Couscous Nuggets

I love fried food. Unfortunately, as you may know, it's no so healthy for you most of the time. In moderation, though, it is acceptable and this recipe is certainly offering a list of healthy ingredients combined together, despite being fried in the pan, so you can still consume some awesome nutrients.

List of Ingredients:

- 2 cup seasoned breadcrumbs
- 3 cups cooked couscous
- 2 cups shredded Gruyere cheese
- Pinch nutmeg
- Pinch cinnamon
- 2 medium eggs
- **Cooking oil (I prefer coconut oil)**

Yield: 4
Cooking Time: **30 minutes**

Instructions:

In a mixing bowl, combine the breadcrumbs, cheese, couscous, nutmeg, and cinnamon.

In a second bowl, whisk the eggs.

Add the eggs to the first mixture and form the nuggets or balls the size you prefer them.

Heat coconut oil in large skillet and fry the nuggets until they are golden and cooked to your satisfaction.

Serve with a salad, as you would a side of bread, or even as an everyday snack.

Recipe 5: Tangy And Sweet Couscous With White Fish

This recipe is awesome to serve to your family and friends. It will certainly make an impression on your guests, but can be a dish you adopt and serve to your family on a regular basis as well, because it is so healthy and certainly yummy.

List of Ingredients:

- 2 cups uncooked couscous
- 2 cups orange juice
- 1 cup water
- Pinch salt
- ½ teaspoons turmeric
- ½ teaspoons cinnamon
- 1 tablespoon red pepper flakes
- 1-pound white fish filets (such as cod, tilapia)
- 2 minced green onions
- 1 can mandarin slices (no sugar added and drained)

- 1 large shredded carrot
- ¼ cup dried raisins
- **Cooking oil**

Yield: 4
Cooking Time: **45 minutes**

Instructions:

Preheat the oven to 400 degrees F. Grease a medium-sized baking dish.

Let's work on cooking the couscous next. In a large saucepan, boil the water and the orange together with salt.

Add the couscous once the liquid is boiling as explained previously in the intro, and remove from the heat. Put the lid on the saucepan and wait until the couscous is done (it should take anywhere between 10-20 minutes for most couscous, but follow the instructions or previous experience to know when it's done. Also use a fork, the grains should feel fluffy).

Meanwhile, you will also place the fish filets in the baking dish, season them with salt, pepper and red pepper flakes. Bake for about 20 minutes.

Also in a skillet, while the couscous is cooking and the fish is baking, you will sauté the green onions and shredded carrot in the cooking oil of your choice.

Add the cooked veggies to the cooked couscous, with the dried raisins, turmeric, cinnamon, and some mandarin slices. Mix well.

When the fish is ready, serve it on a bed of couscous and decorate with additional mandarin slices if you like.

Recipe 6: Baked Stuffed Peppers With Couscous

I think this is a very pleasantly surprising dish to serve anyone you love. Just as you will prepare stuffed peppers with a mixture of rice, cheese, or meat, you can do the same but using cooked couscous with other important key ingredients.

List of Ingredients:

- 4 bell peppers, cut in half (you can choose all same color or mix and match)
- 3 cups cooked couscous
- 2 cups ricotta cheese
- 1 cup shredded parmesan cheese
- 1 small can crushed tomatoes
- ½ teaspoons garlic powder
- ½ teaspoons garlic powder
- **Salt, pepper**

Yield: 4 or 8, depending if you eat 1 or 2 half peppers per person

Cooking Time: **55 minutes**

Instructions:

Preheat the oven to 425 degrees F.

Cut your peppers in half and remove all seeds.

Place the half-peppers face up (you should have 8), on a greased baking dish.

Prepare the stuffing next by combining the ricotta cheese, couscous, tomatoes, and seasonings together in a mixing bowl.

Stuff each pepper with this mixture.

Top off each pepper finally with the shredded parmesan.

Bake in the oven for about 35-40 minutes.

Recipe 7: Fried Couscous With Green Veggies

Don't be shy to use some fresh herbs for this recipe. Cut some from your garden or go to your produce market close by and buy a bunch. Do the same with your green veggies, in this particular recipe I suggest green bell pepper and green onions.

List of Ingredients:

- 1 cup uncooked couscous
- 1 ½ cup turkey broth
- 2 Tablespoons chopped fresh parsley
- 2 Tablespoons chopped fresh chives
- 2 Tablespoons olive oil
- ¼ cup sliced black olives
- 1 cup chopped green bell pepper
- 2 minced green onions
- 2 minced cloves garlic
- ½ teaspoons cumin
- Salt, black pepper
- **Smoked paprika**

Yield: 4

Cooking Time: **40 minutes**

Instructions:

Let's work on cooking the couscous first. In a large saucepan, boil the turkey broth.

Add the couscous once the broth is boiling and cook as usual.

In a large skillet, heat the olive oil and cook the garlic, onions, herbs, and green bell pepper.

Add the cooked couscous to the cooked veggies in the skillet, along with the rest of the ingredients.

Taste the couscous and adjust seasonings if needed, then fry the couscous for another 10 minutes so all ingredients blend well together. Serve warm.

Recipe 8: Chicken Couscous Entree

If you are out of ideas when packing your lunches or lunches for the kids during summer, this is the marvelous recipe to adopt. It will give you the proteins, fibers, vitamins, and minerals you need. The salad does call for chicken, but if you have leftover cooked turkey, it can certainly do just as well.

List of Ingredients:

- 4 cups cooked couscous
- 2 cups cubed or shredded cooked chicken
- 1 medium diced cucumber
- 2 cups cherry tomatoes, cut in halves
- 1 cup crumbled blue cheese
- ¼ cup diced red onion
- ¼ cup Italian dressing of your choice (your favorite store-bought brand or homemade recipe will do perfectly)
- **¼ cup roasted pine nuts**

Yield: 4

Cooking Time: **20 minutes**

Instructions:
Line up all the needed ingredients on your kitchen counter and get ready to assemble.
In a large mixing bowl, dump in the cooked couscous.
Add the Italian dressing and mix well.
Add the rest of the ingredients and combine.
I have tried this recipe with tuna instead of chicken and it is also very good.

Recipe 9: Stuffed Chicken With Couscous And Sundried Tomatoes

This dish is spectacular in presentation and taste. I often choose to make chicken stuffed dishes because I can use brown rice, spinach, or cheeses, but this time I introduce you to the ultimate stuffed chicken. It includes a mixture of couscous, sundried tomatoes and black beans. Just wait to taste it before commenting!
List of Ingredients:

- 4 large chicken breasts (skinless and boneless)
- 2 cups cooked couscous
- 1 can seasoned black beans (rinsed and drained)
- 1 cup chopped sundried tomatoes
- 1 cup sour cream
- Salt, black pepper
- 1 cup shredded parmesan cheese
- ½ teaspoons ground oregano
- ½ teaspoons ground thyme
- **Little olive oil**

Yield: 4
Cooking Time: **50 minutes**

Instructions:
Preheat the oven to 375 degrees F.
Grease a large baking dish and set aside for now.
Clean the chicken breasts and cut in middle, but not all the way, so you have a nice space to stuff the chicken once ready. Set aside.
In a mixing bowl, mix the sour cream, sundried tomatoes, beans, parmesan cheese and spices, herbs.
Stuff each breast with the mixture you just created.
Drizzle a little olive oil on top of chicken and season with salt, and pepper.
Bake in the oven for 40 minutes.
Serve with a side of green veggies.

Recipe 10: Spicy Couscous Soup

You will enjoy this recipe if you like spicy, but also remember if you like milder, you can tone down the spices as well. But this recipe is very much Mexican-style and you can even add a little sour cream on top when serving it. The couscous act as noodles or rice would in any soup.

List of Ingredients:

- 5 cups vegetable broth
- 1 cup sour cream
- 1 large can seasoned diced tomatoes
- 2 cups cooked shredded chicken
- 2 Tablespoons tomato paste
- 1 can seasoned black beans (rinsed and drained)
- 1 cup chopped diced yellow onion
- 1 cup cooked couscous
- ½ teaspoons cumin
- 1 teaspoon smoked paprika
- Salt, black pepper
- **1 tablespoon olive oil**

Yield: 4
Cooking Time: **60 minutes**

Instructions:

Add olive oil to a large saucepan, turn on to medium-heat, and cook the onion for 5 minutes.

Add the diced tomatoes and all seasonings and herbs. Combine well.

Dump in the vegetable broth and the sour cream and stir to mix completely.

Finally, add the cooked chicken and cooked couscous, and combine again.

Keep on medium-low heat for at least 30 minutes until all flavors combine well.

Serve with corn bread.

Recipe 11: Sweet Potatoes With Awesome Couscous Inside

Serving baked sweet potatoes is pretty awesome as it is. However, when you prepare a mixture of couscous with delicious other ingredients and stuff your sweet potatoes with it, you have reached another level of awesomeness! Try it!

List of Ingredients:

- 4 large unpeeled sweet potatoes
- 2 cups cooked couscous
- 1 ½ cup crumbled goat cheese
- ½ cup crumbled bacon bites
- 2 Tablespoons chopped fresh parsley
- 1 tablespoon unsalted butter
- ½ teaspoons cumin
- **Salt, black pepper**

Yield: 4
Cooking Time: 60 minutes or less

Instructions:

You can proceed two different ways. You can bake the sweet potatoes and then stuff them or you can also microwave them and stuff them after. I prefer to use the oven if I have time.

Preheat the oven to 425 degrees F.

Wash the outside of the potatoes without peeling them and place them in a baking dish in the oven for 40 minutes.

Meanwhile, prepare the stuffing by mixing the couscous, goat cheese, bacon bites, parsley, and cumin.

When the baked potatoes are done, cut them in the middle just enough to remove part of the inside, and place that flesh in a spate bowl. Add the butter, salt, and pepper to the potato mixture.

Then combine the potato mixture and the couscous mixture together.

The goat cheese should have melted enough for you to serve the potatoes right away, if not, you can put them back in the oven or microwave for a little while.

Recipe 12: Tomato-Based Couscous Awesome Dish

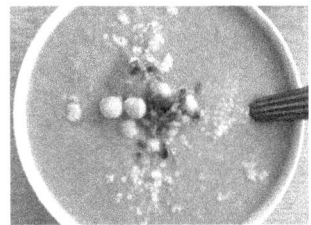

Just because tomato sauces are often served with or combined with pasta, does not mean that it cannot be perfectly matched with couscous. Add some cooked ground meat and you have a really good and quick meal for everyone.

List of Ingredients:

- 2 large cans tomato sauce
- 2 Tablespoons tomato paste
- 4 cups cooked couscous
- 1-pound ground turkey meat
- 1 tablespoon minced garlic
- 1 small chopped yellow onion
- 1 chopped green bell pepper
- 1 tablespoon fresh chopped oregano
- 1 tablespoon dried thyme
- Salt, black pepper
- **1 tablespoon cooking oil**

Yield: 4
Cooking Time: **40 minutes**

Instructions:

Let's start by cooking the ground turkey.

In a large skillet, heat the oil and cook the turkey with the garlic, pepper, and onion. Season with salt and pepper as well.

When the meat is cooked, drain the excess fat and leave in the skillet.

Add the tomato sauce, the tomato paste, and herbs. Combine well with a wooden spoon.

You can proceed 2 different ways.

You can serve this sauce on top of warmed up bed of couscous, or you can combine the couscous with the sauce and serve.

Either way, make sure it's nice and warm.

Recipe 13: Artichoke And Lemon Yummy Couscous Dish

There are a few ways to use artichoke in your dishes. You can decide to use fresh ones or the ones in jars or cans. I prefer to use fresh ones, always when season and time permitting, but for the purpose of this recipe and knowing how busy your lives are, let me keep it simple and use the ones you can purchase on shelves in oil, in the canned vegetables section usually.

List of Ingredients:

- 2 ½ cups low fat turkey broth
- 1½ cups uncooked couscous
- 1 tablespoon avocado oil
- 1 peeled and diced avocado
- 1 cup chopped marinated artichoke hearts
- 2 minced cloves garlic
- 1 small chopped sweet onion
- 2 Tablespoons lemon juice
- 1 tablespoon lemon zest
- 1 tablespoon cayenne pepper

- **Salt, black pepper**

Yield: 4
Cooking Time: **30 minutes**

Instructions:

Let's work on cooking the couscous first. In a large saucepan, boil the turkey broth.

Add the couscous once the broth is boiling and cook as usual.

Meanwhile, in a skillet, add the avocado oil and cook the garlic and sweet onion for about 7 or 8 minutes.

Combine the couscous with the cooked veggies, and the rest of the ingredients, except the avocado.

When serving, place the diced avocado on top of the couscous dish, so it does not get brownish, and perhaps add a little additional lemon juice to avoid brownness as well.

Recipe 14: Cheese, Peas And Couscous

Not only is this side dish lovely to look at, but it is certainly delightful to taste. I think sometimes we underuse peas, and I love sweet peas in this dish with the cheese and couscous, it all mixes so well together, can't really add much more to make it as perfect as can be.

List of Ingredients:

- 2 cups sweet peas
- 2 chopped celery stalks
- 4 cups cooked couscous
- 2 Tablespoons minced mint leaves
- 1 tablespoon lemon juice
- 1 tablespoon lemon zest
- ½ cup chopped yellow onion
- 1 tablespoon minced garlic
- 1 tablespoon olive oil
- Salt, black pepper
- **1 ½ cup crumbled goat cheese**

Yield: 4

Cooking Time: **30 minutes**

Instructions:

In a large skillet or pan, heat the olive oil and cook the yellow onion and garlic for 5-6 minutes.

Add the celery next and continue cooking another 5 minutes.

Dump in the cooked couscous, then add the rest of the ingredients (peas, cheese, seasonings, lemon juice, and lemon zest).

Mix well. You will know it's ready when the goat cheese has started melting and the couscous is becoming almost creamy. Serve warm.

Recipe 15: Gratin Couscous

If you are a cheese lover, you are going to enjoy this recipe for sure! I can't tell you for sure what the best cheeses to use are to complete this recipe. The reason why I am saying this is because everyone prefers different type of cheese, from blue cheese to mozzarella. I will suggest you my favorites and you can always substitute.

List of Ingredients:

- 3 cups cooked couscous
- 1 large shredded zucchini
- 1 large peeled and shredded carrot
- 2 cups vegetable broth
- 2 cups shredded Swiss cheese
- 1 cup sour cream
- ½ cup whole milk
- Pinch nutmeg
- Pinch cinnamon
- **Salt, black pepper**

Yield: 4
Cooking Time: **60 minutes**

Instructions:
Preheat the oven to 400 degrees F.
Grease a medium baking dish and set aside.
Prepare all the ingredients and place the shredded veggies on the very bottom of the dish.
Season them with salt, pepper.
In a bowl, mix the sour cream with the nutmeg, cinnamon, and milk.
Pour on top of the veggies and then add the couscous.
Finish the dish by covering it with a layer of Swiss cheese.
Bake in the oven for 40 minutes and serve warm with grilled chicken or pork.

Recipe 16: Healthy Couscous And Chickpea Casserole

This casserole is as healthy as you get. Use some low-fat mozzarella cheese if you are trying to control how much fat you do use in a recipe. The ingredients listed below mixed together will provide you an excellent source of protein for lunch or dinner any day of the week.

List of Ingredients:

- 3 cups cooked couscous
- 2 cups chickpeas (rinsed and drained really well)
- ½ cup diced red onion
- 2 minced cloves garlic
- 1 tablespoon olive oil
- 1 tablespoon chopped fresh oregano
- 2 Tablespoons fresh chopped parsley
- 1 teaspoon ground coriander
- 2 cups shredded mozzarella cheese
- Salt, black pepper
- 1 large diced seasoned tomatoes (canned)

- **1 tablespoon molasses**

Yield: 4 -6
Cooking Time: **40 minutes**

Instructions:
Preheat oven to 425 degrees F.
Grease a large baking dish and set aside.
In a very large skillet, heat the olive oil and cook the garlic and onion for 5 minutes.
Add the fresh herbs, tomatoes, molasses, and chickpeas, and combine well. Remove from the heat.
Pour the cooked couscous into the baking dish first as the bottom layer.
Add the tomato mixture on top of the couscous.
Finally, the last layer will be the shredded cheese.
Bake in the oven for 30 minutes.

Recipe 17: Very Simple Couscous Recipe

Sometimes simple is the best idea you can have. I like simple as well as I like complicated, or I should say interesting, recipes. This recipe is made to give you a very easy way to cook the perfect side dish any day of the week, without serving something boring.

List of Ingredients:

- 2 minced cloves garlic
- ½ cup diced red onion
- 1 tablespoon lemon juice
- 1 tablespoon lime juice
- 2 cups uncooked couscous
- 3 cups low fat chicken broth
- Salt, black pepper
- Pinch smoked paprika
- **1 tablespoon unsalted butter**

Yield: 4

Cooking Time: **30 minutes**

Instructions:

Let's work on cooking the couscous first. In a large saucepan, boil the chicken broth.

Add the couscous once the broth is boiling and cook as usual.

Now that the couscous is cooked, heat some butter in a large skillet and add the garlic, and red onion and cook for 5 minutes.

Add next the cooked couscous, lemon juice, lime juice, and all seasonings.

Taste and adjust the spices as needed.

Serve as a side dish with meat of your choice.

Recipe 18: Chinese Fried Couscous

What is Chinese fried rice or couscous? In this recipe cookbook, it means it is fried in the skillet with some eggs, veggies, and delicious homemade sauce and seasonings. Much better than any fried rice or couscous you can order for take-out, if you want my opinion.

List of Ingredients:

- 3 cups vegetable broth
- 2 cups uncooked couscous
- 1 tablespoon minced garlic
- 2 cups mixed vegetables (corn, peas, and diced carrots- canned veggies work just fine)
- 1-2 Tablespoons sesame oil
- 2 large eggs
- Salt
- Cayenne pepper
- **Black pepper**

Yield: 4

Cooking Time: **30 minutes**

Instructions:

Let's work on cooking the couscous first. In a large saucepan, boil the vegetable broth.

Add the couscous once the broth is boiling and cook as usual.

If you happen to have left over cooked couscous, then it's even better.

In a skillet, heat the same oil and then cook the garlic for 5 minutes.

Add the eggs, season with salt and pepper, and fry them until done.

Finally, add the cooked mixed veggies and the cooked couscous, as well as the cayenne pepper.

Combine all ingredients very well and continue warming up for 10 minutes before serving.

Recipe 19: Mushrooms And Broccoli Couscous Side Dish

Now let's upgrade to an awesome side dish with more ingredients and more vegetables. I love the combination of broccoli florets and sliced mushrooms in any recipe. You could add chicken to this dish if you would like to add protein and make it a complete meal, but I am suggesting here only veggies for a side dish.
List of Ingredients:

- 3 cups beef broth
- 2 cups uncooked couscous
- 2 cups sliced fresh mushrooms
- 3 cups fresh small or chopped broccoli florets
- 2 minced green onions
- 2 Tablespoons sesame oil
- 1 tablespoon minced garlic
- 1 tablespoon minced ginger
- 1 tablespoon soy sauce
- **¼ cup chopped walnuts**

Yield: 4
Cooking Time: **30 minutes**

Instructions:

Let's work on cooking the couscous first. In a large saucepan, boil the beef broth.

Add the couscous once the broth is boiling and cook as usual.

While the couscous is cooking, heat the oil and soy sauce in a skillet and cook the garlic and ginger for 5 minutes.

Add the mushrooms, green onion, and broccoli, and continue cooking for another 10 minutes.

Finally, serve the warm couscous with the cooked veggies and sprinkle the walnuts on top.

Recipe 20: Scallops And Couscous Perfect Dish

Scallops are one of my favorite seafoods. Especially the large sea scallops, once they are seared, grilled, or sautéed just right, they truly melt in your mouth. Pair the scallops with a yummy couscous dish and you have a winning combination any weekend or week day night. I personally like to drink a glass of dry white wine to match the awesomeness of this dish.

List of Ingredients:

- 1-pound fresh sea scallops
- 3 to 4 cups cooked couscous
- 2 minced cloves garlic
- 2 Tablespoons avocado oil
- 1 diced fresh peeled avocado
- 2 Tablespoons lemon juice
- ¼ cup dry white wine
- ½ teaspoons curry powder
- **Salt, black pepper**

Yield: 4

Cooking Time: **40 minutes**

Instructions:

Make sure to choose your scallops very fresh, from your trusted fish market.

In a skillet, heat the avocado oil and cook the garlic and sea scallops. Season the scallops as you go with the curry powder, salt, and black pepper.

Add the wine 5 minutes before they are done.

Prepare the couscous, dividing it between each plate and get ready to add the scallops on top.

Once the scallops have been added, add the diced avocado and drizzle the lemon juice.

Enjoy without any guilt!

Recipe 21: Quiche-Like Couscous Recipe

This recipe is pretty incredible. It has the look of a quiche, but it's much fluffier and lighter in texture. It is very nutritious and you can certainly as many or as little additional ingredients (veggies or meat) as you like.

List of Ingredients:

- 4 large eggs
- 3 cups cooked couscous
- 1 package plain cream cheese
- 1 cup diced cooked ham
- 1 diced fresh red bell pepper
- 1 cup sour cream
- 1 tablespoon unsalted butter
- 2 minced green onions
- 1 tablespoon minced garlic
- 2 Tablespoons chopped fresh chives
- 2 Tablespoons fresh chopped parsley
- Salt, pepper
- ½ teaspoons ground cumin

- ½ teaspoons ground sage

Yield: 4
Cooking Time: **60 minutes**

Instructions:
Preheat the oven to 425 degrees F.
Grease a pie pan and set aside.
In a large skillet, heat the butter and cook the red bell pepper, onions, and garlic for 10 minutes.
Pour the cooked veggies into a bowl and add all the other ingredients and combine well.
Then pour that mixture into the pie pan and press firmly.
It will look similar to a quiche, but much grainier, of course, because of the couscous.
Bake in the oven for 45 minutes.

Recipe 22: Butternut Squash And Couscous Together

This recipe is also usually easy to concoct during fall, because you can find the butternut squash in your local market and enjoy them just right for a while. Spice up your couscous just right and impress anyone who would taste your famous dish.

List of Ingredients:

- 3 cups coconut milk
- 2 cups uncooked couscous
- 2 cups cooked cubed butternut squash
- ½ chopped red onion
- ¼ cup chopped walnuts
- ¼ cup shredded coconut
- 1 tablespoon lemon juice
- 1 tablespoon lemon zest
- Salt, black pepper
- **½ teaspoons turmeric**

Yield: 4

Cooking Time: **45 minutes**

Instructions:

Let's work on cooking the couscous first. In a large saucepan, boil the coconut milk.

Add the couscous once the coconut milk is boiling and cook as usual.

While the couscous is cooking, prepare all the other ingredients.

If you like you can sauté the squash. I like to keep it as natural as possible, so I cook it ahead of time and just leave it like that.

Once the couscous is cooked and has cooled down, place in a large serving bowl and add all the ingredients. Combine really well.

Taste, as always, and see if you need to adjust the seasonings or not.

Enjoy this wonderful dish with grilled chicken or baked fish perhaps.

Recipe 23: Awesome Couscous And Orange Cake

Here is the first dessert made with couscous we present you in this book (and not the last one). Couscous makes an awesome dessert because it does not have a natural salty taste. Pair it with your favorite almond or vanilla dominant flavor and you are all set for your weekend special dessert for the whole family.
List of Ingredients:

- Cake mixture
- ¾ cup cooked couscous
- 4 eggs
- ¼ cup coconut oil (room temperature)
- ½ cup brown sugar
- 1 cup chopped dates
- 1 cup water
- ½ cup orange juice
- 1 tablespoon orange zest
- 1 cup coconut flour
- 1 teaspoon baking powder

- 1 teaspoon baking soda
- **Pinch salt**

Icing (optional)

- 1 cup confectioner's sugar
- 4 Tablespoons whole milk
- 1 tablespoon water
- **Pinch cinnamon**

Yield: 4
Cooking Time: **40 minutes**

Instructions:
Preheat the oven to 375 degrees F.
Grease a square or round cake pan and set aside.
In a large mixing bowl, mix all the dry ingredients first: flour, baking soda, dates, baking powder, brown sugar, couscous, and salt.
In a second bowl, combine the wet ones: eggs, coconut oil, water, orange juice, and orange zest.
The finally combine both mixtures before pouring into the pie pan.
Bake in the oven for 40 minutes.
When the cake has cooled down you can apply the icing if you like.
To prepare the icing, mix all the listed ingredients and set in the refrigerator until ready to use.

Recipe 24: Cold Couscous Greek Salad

This cold couscous salad reminds me of the one my favorite Lebanese restaurant around the corner form where I used to live in college made. That's why it is one of my favorite recipe in this book, and also of course because it tastes incredible!

List of Ingredients:

- 4 cups cooked couscous
- ½ cup diced red bell pepper
- ½ cup diced green bell pepper
- ¼ cup lime juice
- 1 tablespoon lime zest
- ¼ cup olive oil
- ¼ cup sliced green olives
- 2 cups crumbled feta cheese
- 1 cup fresh diced tomatoes
- Salt, pepper
- ½ teaspoons ground cumin
- 1 teaspoon garlic power
- **1 teaspoon onion powder**

Yield: 4
Cooking Time: **20 minutes**

Instructions:
In a large bowl, pour in the cooked couscous.
In a second bowl, prepare the vinaigrette by mixing the oil, seasonings, lime juice, and lime zest together.
Add the vinaigrette to the couscous and mix well.
Finally, combine all the other List of Ingredients: feta cheese, tomatoes, olives, and peppers.
Serve cold or room temperature.

Recipe 25: Simply Delicious Moroccan Couscous Dish

You can call it a Moroccan-influenced dish or just a mouthwatering couscous dish; either way you would be correct. You can serve it as is as a side dish, or I've even had it as breakfast before. You could also serve it as a full meal and add some protein such as fish, chicken, or grilled pork.

List of Ingredients:

- 3 cups cooked couscous
- ½ cup dried golden raisins
- ½ cup dried cherries
- ½ cup coconut palm sugar
- Pinch ground cinnamon
- Pinch ground nutmeg
- 2 cups cottage cheese (large curds)
- ½ cup chopped pecans
- **3 Tablespoons coconut oil**

Yield: 4
Cooking Time: **20 minutes**

Instructions:
Mix the cooked couscous with the coconut oil, cinnamon, nutmeg, and palm sugar as you would with oatmeal, for example.
Divide the portions in 3-4 bowls.
In a bowl, mix the cottage cheese with the pecans, cherries and raisons and add as a topping in each bowl filled with couscous.
Enjoy!

www.ingramcontent.com/pod-product-compliance
Lightning Source LLC
Chambersburg PA
CBHW071439070526
44578CB00001B/153